ENHANCING CHILDREN'S SOCIAL SKILLS
Assessment and Training

Pergamon Titles of Related Interest

Related Journals
(Free sample copies available upon request)

PSYCHOLOGY PRACTITIONER GUIDEBOOKS

EDITORS
Arnold P. Goldstein, Syracuse University
Leonard Krasner, Stanford University & SUNY at Stony Brook
Sol L. Garfield, Washington University in St. Louis

ENHANCING CHILDREN'S SOCIAL SKILLS
Assessment and Training

JOHNNY L. MATSON
Louisiana State University

THOMAS H. OLLENDICK
Virginia Polytechnic Institute and State University

PERGAMON PRESS
New York · Oxford · Beijing · Frankfurt
São Paulo · Sydney · Tokyo · Toronto

U.S.A.	Pergamon Press, Maxwell House, Fairview Park, Elmsford, New York 10523, U.S.A.
U.K.	Pergamon Press, Headington Hill Hall, Oxford OX3 0BW, England
PEOPLE'S REPUBLIC OF CHINA	Pergamon Press, Room 4037, Qianmen Hotel, Beijing, People's Republic of China
FEDERAL REPUBLIC OF GERMANY	Pergamon Press, Hammerweg 6, D-6242 Kronberg, Federal Republic of Germany
BRAZIL	Pergamon Editora, Rua Eça de Queiros, 346, CEP 04011, Paraiso, São Paulo, Brazil
AUSTRALIA	Pergamon Press Australia, P.O. Box 544, Potts Point, N.S.W. 2011, Australia
JAPAN	Pergamon Press, 8th Floor, Matsuoka Central Building, 1-7-1 Nishishinjuku, Shinjuku-ku, Tokyo 160, Japan
CANADA	Pergamon Press Canada, Suite No. 271, 253 College Street, Toronto, Ontario, Canada M5T 1R5

Copyright © 1988 Pergamon Books Inc.

First edition 1988

Library of Congress Cataloging in Publication Data
Matson, Johnny L.
Enhancing children's social skills.
(Psychology practitioner guidebooks)
Includes indexes.
1. Social skills in children. 2. Behavioral assessment of children. 3. Social skill in children — Study and teaching.
I. Ollendick, Thomas H. II Title. III. Series. [DNLM: 1. Child Guidance. 2. Interpersonal Relations. 3. Personality Assessment — in infancy and childhood. 4. Social Behavior — in infancy and childhood. WS 105.5.S6 M434e]
BF723.S62M37 1988   155.4'18   87-7197

British Library Cataloguing in Publication Data
Matson, Johnny L.
Enhancing children's social skills: assessment and training.
— (Psychology practitioner guidebooks).
1. Child development 2. Social skills
I. Title II. Ollendick, Thomas H.
III. Series
305.2'3   HQ767.9
ISBN 0-08-034308-2 Hardcover
ISBN 0-08-034307-4 Flexicover

Printed in Great Britain by A. Wheaton & Co., Ltd., Exeter

Contents

Preface

The advent of social skills as an important area of study for clinical child psychologists, school psychologists, developmental psychologists, special educators, child psychiatrists, social workers, and other concerned professionals is of relatively recent origin. Since social skills was introduced as a topic for study, there has been a virtual explosion of research and an enhanced awareness of this area as a critical one for attention in clinical research and practice. As witness to these developments, there have been entire issues of journals devoted to this topic in psychology and psychiatry, covering the age span. And, there have been more specialized presentations that focused on various subpopulations such as persons with mental retardation or learning disabilities. All of these developments suggest that social skills as a topic has come "of age" and that it should be influential in the study of children for years to come.

Why has social skills attracted the attention of so many professional groups? The answer seems to be that the topic cuts across the lines of a number of disciplines and theoretical approaches within disciplines. Psychiatry has typically had one generally accepted approach to childhood disorders, while psychology and its subdisciplines have for some time presented a number of avenues concerning the etiology, assessment, and treatment of childhood disorders. Similarly, education has had its own views, and among some subgroups within special education the notion of differential diagnosis and classification which are so integral a part of most psychology and psychiatry programs was in disfavor. The cry, "Label jars, not children," was common. However, the notion that social skills deficits might exist was an appealing idea that has resulted in a common thread that has run across the work of all these professional groups. Furthermore, the research to date has shown that problems in this area are indeed related to many emotional difficulties, other handicapping conditions, and adjustment problems in general.

The current volume is an attempt to draw together the rather impressive literature on children's social skills which has accumulated over the years. A number of developments in how to assess, treat, and even define the inadequacies in social performance have proven both illuminating and informative, and we hope that the reader will be struck with this same sense of evolution. It would seem that social skills as an area of study has been well established and that much of the ground-work has been laid for the development of methods to assess and treat these problems. It will be up to researchers in the future to further study and improve the field. However, not only through the reports of eminent researchers but through the comments of parents, teachers, and other professionals, the topic has not only been well received but endorsed by many. Certainly, this book will not be the last word on social skills training with children. We hope that it will serve as a guide to where we have been, where we are, and where we are likely to be going in social skills training, assessment, and research in the future.

Johnny L. Matson, Ph.D.
Professor of Psychology
Louisiana State University

Thomas H. Ollendick, Ph.D.
Professor of Psychology and
Director of Clinical Training
Virginia Polytechnic Institute
    and State University
Blacksburg, Virginia

Chapter 1

The Role of Social Skills in Childhood Adjustment

INTRODUCTION

Social behavior permeates all aspect of life for children and affects their later adjustment and happiness. A person's ability to get along with others and to engage in prosocial behaviors determines popularity among peers and with teachers, parents, and other significant adults. The degree of social skill is directly related to the number and type of prosocial acts performed by others toward the person evincing social behavior. Furthermore, this behavior has great impact in a number of areas. Social skills or the lack of them has been directly related to rates of juvenile delinquency (Roff et al., 1972), dropping out of school (Ullman, 1975), and in later life, bad-conduct discharges from the military (Roff, 1961) and mental health problems (Cowen et al., 1973). Social skills deficits have been termed a defining characteristic of mental retardation (Grossman, 1983) and deficits in this area are very problematic in visually and hearing impaired children (Matson & Helsel, 1985). With respect to these latter two groups, social skills deficiencies have been linked to major problems in adjustment with peers at school and in the home setting. Similarly, particular personality characteristics and the individual's overall stability seem to be greatly affected by social skills difficulties. For example, Kagan and Moss (1962) have concluded that social interaction anxiety, sex role identification, and patterns of sexual behavior were related to problems in this area. As noted, these deficits can and often do result in lifelong problems (Barclay, 1966; Brown, 1954; Guinouard & Rychlak, 1982). Furthermore, it is not uncommon for negative stereotypes about these children to develop among their peers (Koslin et al., 1986; Sherif et al., 1961).

1

The role of social skills in conduct problems is worth special note. Problems of conduct disorders represent about one-third to one-half of all family and school referrals for mental health services (Gardner & Cole, 1986). Other facts suggest the incredible magnitude of the problem. Conduct disorder is the most common referral to behavior therapists (Robins, 1981); just one form of this disorder, school vandalism, costs $600 million yearly, along with 70,000 serious assaults on teachers (Tygart, 1980). And, unlike many childhood problems which decline with age, antisocial behaviors persist (Olweus, 1979; Shechtman, 1970). Furthermore, many serious problems in adulthood are likely to be associated with earlier conduct disorder and aggression, such as child abuse, battering one's marriage partner, alcoholism, emotional disorders, violent crime, and other social ills. Furthermore, even in childhood, conduct problems may coexist with a number of other problems, including depression, hyperactivity, and learning disabilities (Puig-Antich, 1982; Ross & Ross, 1982).

These data show the pervasive nature of conduct problems, the genesis of which is primarily social in origin. For the teacher or clinician, the serious nature of this social skills deficit is self-evident. This recognition may account in part for the widespread popularity of social skills training and research.

Yet another problem is the relationship of social skills to various forms of psychopathology. Much of the early social skills treatment and assessment research with adults focused on the effects of social skills training on schizophrenic persons. Most prominent among these researchers have been Hersen and Bellack (1976), who have demonstrated in numerous studies with chronic schizophrenics that increasing adaptive social behaviors markedly improves the person's adaptation to the community. Similar problems have been noted with respect to social behaviors and depression. Among the persons who popularized this relationship are Lewinsohn (1975) and Beck and associates (Beck et al., 1978). Social withdrawal and self-motivated isolation are among the behaviors that these persons exhibited. Lewinsohn (1975) in particular has addressed this problem directly with the development of a training component of his treatment for depression in adults that was aimed specifically at teaching proper social skills along with recording these adaptive responses as they occurred. The value of this approach and the overlap of these problem areas in children has been confirmed empirically by Helsel and Matson (1984). These researchers found a strong relationship between social behaviors and depression in children 4 to 10 years of age. Similarly, they found that there were considerable differences in these groups by age.

It is also likely that subtypes of childhood depression exist and that the type and severity of social skills deficits that exists and their severity may be altered considerably. Much more research is needed to further describe these phenomena. This area of research is still a relatively new one ; there are far fewer researchers in clinical child psychology and child psychiatry than is the case for mental health professionals working with adults. Therefore it may be some time before these problems can be resolved. Fortunately, developmental psychologists, school psychologists, social workers, and special educators have also become involved in the social skills area and have been instrumental in advancing research and practice.

With children, more so than adults, the nature of how social skills develop is an important consideration. Children who are unacceptable to their peers may be deprived of a number of important experiences, and this may lead to further maladaptation (Bierman & Furman, 1984). These considerations harken back to theories such as those of Kohlberg (1973), who addressed the issue of stages of moral development. From the skills building theorectical perspective, these responses could be viewed as particular social behaviors that are developed through modeling, practice, and reinforcement. In addition to moral reasoning, some researchers have described other theoretical constructs which may fit into the social skills paradigm. These are altruism, avoidance of conflict, learning to reinforce others, and enhancing peer acceptance (Asher et al., 1977).

Since the child's behavior does not occur in isolation, we must consider the interactional effects of social behavior with the variations in behavior based on the responses of others. The behavior of two primary interactional groups — the peer group and the family — can, to a large degree, determine what and how social skills training for the targeted child should be performed. It has been suggested that gaining peer acceptance may be directly related to social skills adequacy (Combs & Slaby, 1977). However, negative views of the child may develop over time, thus, the more unskilled and less popular the child, the more difficult it may be to overcome these stereotypes (Koslin et al.m, 1986; Sherif et al., 1961). The other potential problem group of greatest concern is the family. It has been found, for example, that marital discord and child behavior problems are closely related (Emery, 1982; O'Leary & Emery, 1985) and may be due either to the child or to the parents' reciprocal relationship (Forehand et al., 1986). Thus, the child's behavior must be studied broadly, and treatment often may need to be given in a family context.

We hope the reader has been intrigued by what has been presented up to this point — namely, that a large number of areas of the child's present and future life are related to appropriate social functioning.

However, it is also important to stress that the severity of problems that may accrue due to social skills deficits is considerable. Persons who evince these problems to a large degree may, as previously noted, experience increased adjustment problems as they get older, producing a snowball effect that can result in minimal adaptive functioning in adulthood. These persons may, as a result, become unproductive members of society and, as such, become a drain on the resources of society. The cost in psychological and physical suffering as well as the overall negative financial and social cost can be considerable for those persons affected.

It should be pointed out that these effects are not just for isolated cases; the magnitude of the problem is considerable. Gronlund (1959), for example, found that 12% of children in normal classrooms reported having only one friend, while 6% of children reported having no friends at all. Hymel and Asher (1977) have replicated this study, with similar results. Related to these data are findings that social withdrawal, often defined as passive and slow in speech, has also been a frequently reported problem (Gottman, 1977; Patterson, 1964). Obviously, these data provide reason for concern on the part of the professional.

Unlike other problem areas, extremes in either direction can be evident with social skills. Aggression and conduct problems, as well as social withdrawal and isolation, are frequent with children. Conduct disorders are the most frequent reason for children — by and large males — being referred by school personnel to psychologists and social workers (Gardner & Cole, 1987). Similarly, conduct problems seem to be particularly recalcitrant to treatment; often, the long-term prognosis is worse than what is seen with many severe forms of psychopathology.

It is evident from these problems that social skills are likely to effect a very broad range of psychological response patterns. It seems then that attention is required from a variety of professional disciplines to help remediate these very frequent social/interpersonal problems. Most certainly educators would be among those who should be acquainted with these problems and be involved with their solution. Similarly, clinical psychologists, school counselors, and child psychiatrists are likely to encounter these social skills deficits in almost every child with whom they have professional contact. Given the magnitude and severity of these problems, it would seen that social skills deficits should be seen not only as a major part of the underlying etiology of emotional, personality, and adjustment problems of children but as an area where efforts may have very beneficial preventative effects as well. Therefore, not only will definitions of the problem and settings where these deficits occur be reviewed, but issues in the early identification of social difficulties will be discussed.

WHAT ARE SOCIAL SKILLS?

There has been some confusion concerning what exactly social skills are and how they should be defined. The positive feature of this confusion has been that a broad group of professional disciplines (e.g., social work, education, special education, school psychology, developmental psychology, clinical psychology, psychiatry, and psychiatric nursing) have been interested in studying and developing solutions for this problem. Similarly, persons with a number of theoretical orientations have had interest in this topic, including behavioral and developmental psychologists, school psychologists, psychiatrists, and educators. Among the behavioral groups there have also been a number of subtypes, including operant conditioning social learning theory, and cognitive behavior therapy. These theories will be reviewed later.

A final problem has been the confusion that has resulted due to the various types of subpopulations of children that have been studied and treated. With the general childhood population, interpersonal skill has been the typical definition that has been used. In the case of mentally retarded persons, however, the definition of social skills has been expanded to include an inordinate number of behaviors, including dressing and hygiene skills. These behaviors do not fit a definition of social skills that would be best with respect to consistency across the broad range of populations that have received treatment. However, it does point out the confusion that has existed among persons working in the field as a whole.

Assuming that the narrower definition of interpersonal responses is used, what specifically are these interpersonal behaviors and what are the parameters of these responses? A brief review of these two issues will follow. They are of considerable importance given that they have been major topics for research and clinical practice.

It should be kept in mind that the socially skilled person is one who can adapt well to his or her environment and who can (particularly in the case of children) avoid conflict of both a verbal and physical nature through communications with others. On the other hand, the socially unskilled person is said to often engage in conduct problems such as fights with other children, is unpopular with peers and adults, and does not get along well with his or her teacher or other professionals. This child is also frequently perceived as being uncaring about the rights and privileges of others and as being very self-centered in his or her behavior. Many of the behaviors that fall within the general rubric of conduct disorder have been quantified in the social skills literature. Children with poor social skills that have implications for conduct problems often do not follow the accepted rules of society and receive attention for socially unacceptable behavior such as cursing, talking back to adults, arguing with peers, and refusing to recognize the rights of others (for example, refusing to take turns or always "cutting ahead" on the lunch line).

The socially skilled person — that is, the person who learns to perform social skills or is motivated to evince social skills already in his or her repertoire — can have many positive implications. This person is much more likely to receive the types of reinforcers that most of us would view as socially acceptable. These reinforcers can operate on a range of parameters and are described well by Kelly (1982). A brief review of each of these parameters will follow.

The first category mentioned by Kelly as a benefit of social skills training is the building of relationships. The purpose of relationship building is to establish friendships with others and to sustain existing relationships. It should be pointed out that this goal is even more critical for children if we look at this issue from a development level, since these young people are in the process of learning how to get along with others. It is also important to note that children engage in much of their relationship building through nonverbal behaviors.

Play and other nonverbal responses should be monitored as closely as possible for the child to get along with peers. It is also important for the child to learn to discriminate how to build relationships with adults as compared to children. Obviously, the skills that are needed to deal with grownups vary considerably from what one needs to do with other children and even among adults. The needed skills may be quite different (e.g., teacher versus parent). The reader can see that this is a very complex issue for the child; it should be kept in mind that the child may do well with one group of persons and not the others. Evaluating these problem areas is a major topic of concern for the clinician, teacher, and parent.

Second, social skills may also bring about secondary gains. Thus, for example, the child may mind the teacher in class so that he or she may get a good grade in deportment, which may prove to be pleasing to the parent. This skill is important in that it translates to social skills that the child may need as an adult. For example, the salesperson in a store will attempt to be pleasant to a potential buyer not so much for the purpose of making a friend but rather as a way of obtaining a purchase which provides him or her a commission, which results in a larger pay check. For most of us, this monetary reward would be a positive outcome. This type of secondary gain is something that we engage in almost daily.

A third and perhaps most important category of social skills for children to master is the ability to handle the unreasonable behavior of others. Children who typically get in trouble at school and home with respect to social interpersonal skills are poor in their ability to deal with the inappropriate social behaviors of others. For example, if another child teases the individual or makes derogatory statements, how does the person react? Obviously, it may be difficult to eliminate all problems that can result in conflict, but in many instances the child's responses markedly escalate the seriousness of the situation. In reviewing the social skills literature, it should come as no great surprise that the conduct-disordered child is particularly poor in his or her ability to deal with these types of situations. The problem is compounded by the fact that the child may derive reinforcement from his or her closest friends for making derogatory comments or fighting with others. Similarly, the home environment may be such that behaviors of this type are encouraged.

Knowing the situations where social skills should be used is another area that deserves attention. This problem is particularly great with young children who are mentally retarded, since in many cases they do not have the necessary skills that should be performed in various situations. Typical of this problem is the small child who tells Grandpa that Mommy said she wished he would get rid of that ugly old winter coat that he wears all the time. Stories of this type, which are embarrassing to the parents, are of course common, due to the child's failure to discriminate properly. Another group that has particular problems in this situation includes persons with major physical difficulties, such as hearing or visual impairments. These persons cannot pick up on the same cues that others can attend to; as a result it may be difficult for them to discriminate among social situations, particularly if very fine visual or auditory discriminations are required. Also, these children tend to be particularly immature for their age, further compounding this situation (Matson & Helsel, 1986).

A final problem area to be discussed is the failure to display skills that the child has in his repertoire. One study performed at the University of Pittsburgh clearly demonstrates this motivational problem. The children in the study were between 6 and 12 years old. Sixteen children on a psychiatric inpatient unit received a positive event prior to social skills assessment. Sixteen matched children did not receive a positive event prior to assessment (Kazdin et al., 1982). Those who had the positive event prior to assessment performed better. These results were replicated under different conditions. In a study by Kazdin et al., (1981), two groups — one comprised of normal and one of psychiatrically impaired children — were reinforced for doing their best while the other group was not. Those who were rewarded performed much better. These data suggest that mood and rewards for performance may be important factors in social skills.

It should be evident to the reader that appropriate social skills are of considerable importance. However, the concern over social skills and other mental health issues is of only recent origin. The historical development of mental health services for children will constitute the next issue for discussion.

HISTORICAL DEVELOPMENTS

The area of childhood development and emotional problems is of recent origin when compared to the written history of mankind or even the short history of psychopathology and adjustment problems. Thus, while references to psychopathology can be dated to prehistoric times (Ollendick & Hersen, 1983; Schwartz & Johnson, 1981), the concept with children is of more recent origin. In general, during the Greek and Roman periods, persons who were deranged, were adjusted poorly to the community, or had serious physical or sensory handicaps were ridiculed, banned from society, or worse. During the Dark Ages, demonology was a strongly held belief; it was felt that persons deserved what they got and that a handicap or psychosis was a punishment from God. Thus, no real attempt to treat problem children was forthcoming. Martin Luther, one of the great religious reformers, felt that deranged persons should be burned at the stake. To further compound the problems, it was not generally recognized that children had different thought processes than adults or even that mental development occurred. Children were in effect treated as small adults, yet they were also viewed as the property of their parents. Furthermore, there were no child-protection provisions in the laws of most European countries and children were forced to work at a very young age. All of these factors led to very unpleasant situations for children at that time.

The 18th and early 19th centuries saw the first systematic attempts to resolve the mental health and adjustment problems of children. Many of these early developments can be credited to educators of the period. For example, Froebel (1903) founded the first kindergarten and applied the discovery method of education to the very young. Perhaps even more importance were the early ideas of Herbart (1901) who introduced the concept that children advance through various stages of cognitive development, an area that has become one of the most heavily researched in the entire field of psychology. Given the view that children had the same basic cognitive processes as adults, the recognition of intellectual differences based on normal development was a major step in advancing the concepts of child psychology and education.

The 19th century also saw a number of very important developments. The recognition that even children with major social and genetic deprivation could be helped to at least some degree was realized. The classic case was that of the Wild Boy of Aveyron, who had grown up in the wilderness with hardly any contact with humans. Itard, a French physician, took this boy and attempted to educate him. This attempt, while not particularly effective, at least developed interest in possible treatments.

In the United States the interest in childhood disorders began to receive attention soon after the American and French Revolutions. While the information often lacked a sufficient data base, they did demonstrate the growing interest in this problem (Swanson & Reinert, 1979). Efforts in this area dealt primarily with classification and education based on academic performance, or in some cases the identification of children with adjustment problems. The information generated was general and there was no specific data base. It is only within the last 20 years that a major taxonomy of childhood psychopathology has begun to emerge and social skills research has begun to flourish. The developments in this area have been significant and rapid and will be reviewed next.

The history of social skills and its development as a popular area for consideration by professionals began primarily with research on adults. Work with children followed shortly thereafter and has become increasingly popular. A major advantage of social skills work is that it cuts across a wide range of professional disciplines, providing a common language to researcher, clinicians, and teachers. It has broad applicability since it relates to most emotional and adjustment problems of children (Ollendick & Cerny, 1981).

The developments of a conceptual basis for social skills training came out of social learning theory. Similarly, the treatment modalities that have been used have been primarily based on this theoretical notion. The idea was that many of the responses that help us adapt to our environment and those around us are learned behaviors. It is generally assumed that observations of others greatly determine the types of response that we are likely to display and the behaviors that prove to be successful. These behaviors are reinforced and therefore are likely to be those which we continue to perform.

The treatment of these problems in a manner that can be supported by experimental verification is a recent phenomenon, with the first studies appearing in this context was with adults and dealt specifically with assertiveness. Typical of this research were studies that emphasized social learning treatment methods in the amelioration of college males' fear and general inability to ask females for dates (McFall & Lillesand,

1971; McFall & Marston, 1970). Assertiveness training for women also became a popular notion (Richey, 1981). In both of these lines of research, the emphasis was on teaching appropriate assertiveness. That is, a person could be viewed as overly passive or overly aggressive, depending on the particular social context in which the response was made and whether the person was male or female. A number of other demographic behaviors also proved to be important. For example, an employee who tends to be less outspoken with his or her employer than his or her children may be adaptive in social functioning. This problem is perhaps of even greater complexity with children when it is considered that their behavior is typically viewed as being more appropriate if it is passive with adults. Also, it should be kept in mind that the particular values of a family may markedly affect the degree, type, and quality of these interactions.

The emphasis on assertive behaviors of college men and women, while still considered important, soon gave way in the research literature to a much broader interpretation of social skills deficits. The latter term referred to assertiveness but also to a large number of other problem behaviors that were interpersonal in context. Researchers and clinicians began to think of social skills as a quantity of behavior that could be inappropriate in extremes, either too frequent or infrequent, depending on the person or situation. For example, when asked a question an individual could give an answer that was one word or the response could take an hour. Either or these extremes would be inappropriate in most situations.

The focus also changed from generally normal persons who were having minor adjustment problems to persons with serious emotional problems. This development was encouraging and probably due to the power and effectiveness of the technology. The application of these procedures to more severe populations was best exemplified by the work of Hersen and Bellack, who did a great deal of research with chronic schizophrenic patients.

A term first used by Zigler and Phillips (1962), "premorbid social competence, " was frequently used to describe these seriously disturbed persons, stressing the relationship of serious mental illness and the inability to adjust due to very poor interpersonal skills. The potential preventive nature of social skills training also became a major rationale for this type of patient; the reader may recall that this issue has been alluded to with respect to children. Similarly, chronic schizophrenics were found to relapse much more frequently if they were returned to families that were highly socially dysfunctional (Liberman et al., 1982). These points are strong arguments for social skills training.

Two examples of social skills should be sufficient to give the reader an idea of how rapidly expansion has occurred. Hersen and Bellack (1976) worked with persons who had been hospitalized several times, usually for 90 days or less. The problems these persons experienced were broken down into discrete social behaviors such as eye contact, quality of speech, content of speech, appropriateness of affect, speech latency, and other specific behaviors. These persons were treated using behavioral strategies in an effort to improve their ability to tolerate others. The hypothesis was that the individual did not possess the necessary skills to function in an acceptable interpersonal fashion.

A second group of researchers at UCLA, directed by Robert Paul Liberman, used a similar methodological approach. Their efforts have involved employing antipsychotic medications — an approach which is generally viewed as the treatment of choice in conjunction with behavior therapy (Liberman & Davis, 1975). Additionally, they have focused on the home environment and regulating what they call expressed emotions of the afflicted person and his or her family. The work of this group and other researchers who are working with these adult populations is beginning to look at the differing forms of schizophrenia, the course of the disorder, and how best to promote generalization (Liberman et al., 1982).

The efficacy of social skills training and its popularity and effectiveness in treating chronic schizophrenia resulted in this method also being used with depression in adults. Lewinsohn and his associates at the University of Oregon were perhaps the first to recognize and formulate a theoretical model for the treatment of depression which emphasized social skills deficits and excesses as a primary treatment component. They postulated that large amounts of positive reinforcement in the depressed person's environment are not used to the best possible advantage. This situation is the case because of the general social withdrawal which is evident and because a primary function of treatment is reestablishing pleasurable experiences by the contingent reinforcement of appropriate social behaviors (Liberman & Davis, 1975). In a number of experiments they determined a relationship between the frequency of pleasant activities and mood (Lewinsohn & Graf, 1973; Lewinsohn & Libert, 1972). In addition to the positive effects noted in these studies, it has been found that normally adjusted persons engage in more pleasurable activities than persons with depression. This conceptualization, particularly for unipolar depressives, has become a popular one. Several groups of investigators have been doing research in this area and have largely confirmed Lewinsohn's assumptions. Similarly, in a large controlled treatment outcome study, Hersen et al., (1980) found that social skills training led not only to improved interpersonal functioning but to significant reductions in vegetative symptoms of unipolar nonpsychotic persons. Much activity seems to be occurring in this area of psychopathology research, and much more experimentation with, and advances in, this area are likely in the next few years.

Given the success of social skills treatment with adults and its general relationship to a fairly broad range of problems, it is no wonder that social skills programs with children also became popular. There is no need to go into a history of this problem, since research in the area is of such recent origin. However, it is likely that much of the clinical work now going on was stimulated by the successes that have been noted with respect to college students, women's assertiveness, chronic schizophrenia, and depression.

While the history of social skills training is very short, this situation also holds for the general area of childhood psychopathology and adjustment. Although training has been used with education problems for some time, the techniques that were applied tended not to have a systematic base, nor did they have a consistent theoretical underpinning. It is only within the last 30 years that well-defined and specified assessment and treatments have been developed. Largely, these have been within the general purview of operant conditioning or social learning theory.

The research on social skills has been largely with mentally retarded, learning disabled, or emotionally disturbed children. Oftentimes this work has been related to the improvement of school adjustment or to further enhance mainstreaming and/or normalization. Most of the initial research was done by psychologists with an applied behavior analysis background. Most of these professionals were trained in an operant laboratory, doing animal research. Thus, the research that emerged was an extension of the operant tradition. Persons with this background are still doing social skills research, but the research has become more diffuse, with professionals in clinical child psychology, school psychology, developmental psychology, and special education contributing substantially to the literature. Each of these groups has taken a somewhat different approach to the problem; this is viewed as a particularly healthy development, since it has resulted in a much more diverse approach with a greater range of theoretical views and available assessment and treatment strategies. Each of these approaches to the topic will be discussed briefly.

Clinical child psychologists have typically emphasized persons with more serious problems, to the extent that these individuals have been referred for treatment in an outpatient mental health clinic or the children have been hospitalized. Among the hospital settings that have been reported in research studies on the topic, the most typical have been inpatient units of large university medical schools or institutions for mentally retarded or psychiatrically impaired persons. University programs tend to be small, 5 to 25 beds, with children staying approximately 60 to 90 days. The movement toward treatment in the least restrictive environment has had a major impact. Also, money has become a major issue. Patient stays used to be much longer, but the development of new insurance guidelines on maximum payments of psychiatric hospitalization has greatly affected the approach to care. The 90-day limit is usually adhered to very closely since hospitalizations tend to be very expensive $600 to $800 per day not being uncommon. Of course, the number and professional training of the staff tends to be extraordinarily high. Often there are two staff per child, although the staffing ratios are spread out over three shifts. Thus, the treatments and assessments that are used tend to be very elegant and highly effective. A major criticism of this approach, however, is that most facilities do not have the trained staff or the numbers to duplicate these programs. Also, generalization is often a problem when a child changes treatment settings. Thus, one must consider how effective the treatment component may be over time. This area is one that requires additional study.

State hospitals are the second inpatient setting where clinical child psychologists frequently work. These facilities tend to be very large, often housing 500 to 1,000 patients. Unfortunately, facilities of this sort typically do not have the high staffing ratios associated with medical centers, and thus the type and sophistication of the programs are compromised somewhat. Also, the hospitalized persons are, on average, more severely disturbed and their problems are more chronic than those of persons placed in medical centers. As a result, the focus of treatment tends to differ in many instances. Rather than primarily conducting a diagnostic and treatment workup, treatment is begun but followed up in the community. In the institution the emphasis is often on trying to enhance adjustment — often in very minimal ways, including getting along better with other patients and attending to basic hygiene care, since the clients are so severely impaired. Furthermore, the institutionalized persons are likely to be on psychotropic medications due to the nature and chronic course of their problems. Thus, the treatment of social skills in the latter case is likely to focus on enhancing basic skills and the maintenance of existing ones. Conversely, children seen in the medical school situation on an inpatient basis are more likely to be experiencing adjustment problems that have not been clearly identified previously. In addition to having less recalcitrant problems, it is also likely that they are not on, nor have they been on, psychotrophic medications. Thus, to some degree the behavior problems these children experience may be more amenable to treatment than is the case with the adult populations.

The school psychologist, developmental psychologist, and special educator are more likely to be working with children who have not developed problems so severe as to warrant hospitalization or outpatient psychological treatment. However, the philosophy of treatment may differ to some degree from one of these disciplines to another. Moreover, the school psychologist in most cases will not be in a position to provide services directly. Given the large number of children for whom the school psychologist is responsible — typically, two to four schools and perhaps as many as 900 children — this approach is not feasible, even if only 5% to 10% of the children are experiencing social skills deficits. Additionally, school psychologists are also responsible for doing a large number of psychological assessments, which may vary from standard intellectual assessments to evaluations of academic achievement to evaluations of emotional problems. Thus, it is not surprising that those professionals within school psychology advocate the use of their work time for the development of treatment plans as well as assessing problem behaviors within a consultative model. This emphasis seems to be growing and as such shows a movement of school pyschology from a field primarily geared to assessment toward an intervention model of professional services.

With this approach the school psychologist would serve primarily as a trainer and provider of backup support for the teacher, who would provide the child's treatment. This approach might consist of the school psychologist doing an initial assessment, helping the teacher develop a treatment plan, and then allowing the training to be done either by reinforcement of the behaviors during the day in routine classroom situations, or in social skills groups that might take up 30 minutes to an hour three to five times weekly during the regular school day. These meetings could be followed by a weekly meeting with the school psychologist to review progress.

The development psychologist takes a somewhat different view. The emphasis in this research has been on the differences in social responding across age group. Obviously, what is considered acceptable social responding for a 6-year-old would not be the same as for a 12-year-old. Similarly, the popularity of children as perceived by other children and the issue of the effects peers have on their behavior over time has been a major issue for research. Most of the emphasis has been on the school and home environment. While these persons have not been as involved in the direct provisions of services, their efforts have been instrumental in identifying developmental issues that are of clear importance in the assessment and treatment of children.

Special educators have been particularly active in recent years with respect to social skills training. Unlike regular educators, these teachers typically have classes of 8 to 15 students and a teacher's aide. The regular classsroom teacher, on the other hand, may have 20 to 30 students with the same amount of help. Thus, assessment and training of social skills is more feasible with special education populations in the school setting. Secondly, most (90% to 98%) children in special education classes have social interpersonal problems; the fact that they are having academic and/or emotional problems further exacerbates the situation. The skills that are trained may vary tremendously depending on the skill and cognition level of the persons to be trained. Many learning disabled children may have great potential and very few deficits. On the other hand, persons in the severe and profound range of mental retardation may have serious visual, hearing, or physically handicapping limitations. In these instances the development of social skills curricula has been slow in coming. The emphasis in special education has been to make the development social skills a part of the curriculum. Thus, special class time is set aside and the special education program itself is geared toward goals such as getting along better with other children and acquiring the skills needed to do so. In the case of children with major cognitive deficits resulting in their classification as severely or profoundly mentally retarded, social skills training may constitute orientation responses of the eyes to persons that are talking or smiling at others. While these may seem like small gains to many individuals, such responses prove to be very gratifying to parents, siblings, and many teachers. Thus, the range and scope of social skills training has expanded markedly in recent years.

SUMMARY

A more detailed description of various special populations will follow later. Suffice it to say that we are supportive of the concept of "zero reject" with respect to social skills training of children (Matson & Mulick, 1983). It should be mentioned that there are basically four settings in which social skills training is most likely to occur with a wide range of children. These include clinic or hospital settings, the home, the school, or the community. To date, the published research has primarily emphasized the clinic, hospital, and school as settings for intervention. This evolution of course makes sense, since these are the places where professionals most frequently see children and have a good deal of control over children's behavior. It is likely that this particular emphasis will continue. However, it should be pointed out that the performance of social skills is probably more important in the home and community for the majority of children who receive social skills training. Similarly, training carried out in these settings is likely to markedly improve the child's behavior in the other settings noted above.

A review of social skills as a general topic area and its relationships to a wide range of emotional disorders has been discussed. Also, it should be strongly emphasized that attending to the social skills excesses and deficits may be a very important issue, particularly with children. Another consideration in social skills training is that this terminology cuts across a number of disciplines and subdisciplines such as education, various specialities in psychology, and child psychiatry and pediatrics. The reader should recognize that behavior therapy is the primary theoretical approach to treatment in the area of social skills. A number of subareas within this general theoretical framework have been described; these and related theoretical issues will constitute the main emphasis of the next chapter.

Chapter 2
Behavioral Assessment

INTRODUCTION

An important consideration for improving social behavior is the accurate identification of skills in this specific response class. Most of the procedures used in pursuit of this goal can be characterized as behavioral assessment, although some of the more recent measures use classic test development properties as well. The particular techniques that are used fall under the categories of role-playing, direct behavioral observations, self-report questionnaires, and self-ratings (Nelson et al., 1985). While most assessors have applied only one or two of these techniques, using several social skills assessment approaches can be beneficial as a means of establishing multiple cutoff criteria. This method is advisable wherever possible. It stands to reason that using several methods of assessment will enhance the likelihood of obtaining data that is both comprehensive and representative of the problem to be studied with respect to specifically affected areas of social performance and related collateral behaviors. A study by Nelson et al. (1985) supports this assumption, although it should be pointed out that the subjects were college students. They used four behavioral assessment techniques, including role-playing, interviews, questionnaires, and self-ratings. These investigators found that ratings differed not only by the types of assessment techniques used but also by the social situation where the interaction occurred. Similar conclusions for children were reached by Ollendick (1981).

The sensitivity to conditions of assessment have also been demonstrated in a series of studies with children. We highly recommend that the educator and clinician be sensitive to this issue, since as will be described, many procedural phenomena typically discounted in assessment can have profound effects. In one such study where preassessment conditions were examined, Kazdin et al. (1982) evaluated 32 children ages 6 to 12 who were psychiatric inpatients at a large medical school. Twenty-six of the children studied were male and six were female. Two assessment methods were employed: a behavioral role-play test and a self-confidence questionnaire. One or two alternative forms of each measure was employed at each of two assessment periods separated by 20 minutes. The entire assessment phase took about one hour to complete. In the period separating the pretest and posttest, half of the children were randomly assigned to a condition where no event was scheduled during the interval between assessments. A second, alternate condition involved events which occurred in the interval between the two assessments. For the positive induction group, each child was to complete a maze. The mazes were selected so that they could be completed easily, thus ensuring a positive experience. Each child was told that by successfully completing the maze he or she would be allowed to select a prize which remained in the child's sight while he or she was working on the maze. This strategy was used so that a visual reminder of the reinforcement would be present. In fact, no criteria were set for correct responding; therefore, whatever the child did, (s)he was rewarded. When the tangible reinforcer was given, lavish praise by the adult supervising the work on the maze was also provided. These evaluators were also responsible for supervising the social skills assessment. Role-play performance and measures of self-confidence demonstrated greater improvements for the positive experience group.

These data should be of interest to the educator, since it is evident that these events can affect performance in a substantial way. Also, the results should suggest that the testing environment needs to be strictly controlled or highly misleading results may occur. Other studies support this assumption. It has been shown, for example, that the extent and purpose for which the behavior is assessed can *markedly affect the results* (e.g., the home, school, a psychological clinic). Bernstein and Nietzel (1977) found that if clients were led to believe that their performance was being evaluated for treatment purposes in which children are instructed to minimize their anxiety or are led to believe anxiety will diminish lead to significant changes (Bernstein, 1973; Borkovec, 1973). Unfortunately, in most clinical settings these variables are not taken into account.

Another example specific to the assessment of social skills in children and to the sensitivity of these measures was reported by Kazdin et al. (1981). They treated 30 hospitalized psychiatric patients and 30 children matched on age and sex from a local laboratory school. Three assessment methods were employed, including a knowledge questionnaire, behavioral role-play tests, and a self-efficacy questionnaire. One of two assessment occasions separated by an interval of approximately one week was employed. Following a pretest, half of the children were told they would be reinforced for doing their best. The reinforcement was not provided for any specific response. Children in the reinforcement condition performed differently compared to children who were not reinforced. The incentive (reinforcement) condition was equally effective with psychiatrically disturbed children and "normals" matched in age, gender, and race. It is of note that a considerable amount of social skills training has been conducted on the assumption that a client does not possess the requisite skills. These data suggest that often the person may not perform the desired skills, not because of lack of knowledge or the skill to do so; rather, the child may not perform the required skills due to lack of motivation. While this point may seem like a reasonable and easily recognised one, it is often overlooked.

Given knowledge of the sensitivity of assessment, the clinician or educator should consider several points in conducting social skills assessment. First, when individual or small-group assessments are conducted, the maintenance of a highly standardized environment and testing conditions is required. Second, given the affective nature of behaviors assessed, an effort to be pleasant to the child and try to enhance higher motivation is critical. Third, some sort of social and tangible reward for small children, and social and other appropriate rewards for older youth, should be considered. This approach should be important for increasing the likelihood that skill levels already in the person's repertoire are produced. Many times children who are not assessed using these procedures are assumed not to possess skills which they indeed have. Obviously, a careful assessment on this dimension can save a considerable amount of unnecessary training time for children who are not performing up to their capabilities on social skills assessments.

ASSESSMENT TECHNIQUES

In addition to ensuring that adequate safeguards are in place for accurate assessment, a good deal of research on the development of instruments and other techniques has been performed. Among the most commonly employed procedures have been checklists, socimetric ratings, role-playing scenes, and direct observation of in vivo social situations. Each of these approaches has advantages and disadvantages and may account in part for the frequent recommendation to use multiple assessment methods (Ollendick & Hersen, 1984). Therefore, the reader should be familiar with the range of available techniques, their reliability and validity, and the available empirical support across subpopulations for each method. In addition, limitations with respect to staff, settings in which the assessment occurs, and where later training is likely to happen will be reviewed.

Checklists

Checklists are a traditional and common form of assessment for a range of childhood problems. A number of developments in this area are specific to social skills in children. Also, some efforts have been made to tailor social skills checklists to particular settings. A review of each scale and its likely applications will be provided in the next few pages.

The Matson Evaluation of Social Skills with Youngsters (MESSY) has been the most heavily researched social skills checklist with children. The initial sample studied included 744 children and youths between 4 and 18 years of age. They were tested in private and public schools in the Midwest (Matson et al., 1983). Two samples were drawn from the original list, with 422 children randomly assigned to a self-report group and 322 children being rated by their teacher. Initially, the scale had 92 items, selected from general scales of psychopathology, behaviors targeted in social skills studies with children, and clinical observations and discussions with professionals who worked with children. Inter-rater reliability of the target behaviors was computed, decreasing the number of items to 62 for the self-report version and 64 for the teacher/parent report. (See Tables 1.1 and 1.2.)

In developing a rating scale for social skills in children, a number of factors must be considered. These issues include the evaluation of a wide range of verbal and nonverbal behaviors which indicate interpersonal effectiveness (Rinn & Markle, 1980). Also, behaviors should be sufficiently precise so that they can serve as targets for interventions, and they should ensure the maximizing of reinforcing situations and level of reinforcement in already existing reinforcing situations. Further, the reliability and validity of the items should be demonstrated. In such an attempt for the MESSY, the test-retest reliability was found to be high. Also, the two versions of the scale were factor analyzed and the factors were then labeled. This initial study was useful in establishing the basic psychometric properties of the scale.

The MESSY may also be valuable when conducting social skills assessments and determining their relationship to other variables. One

Table 2.1. First-Order Varimax Loadings on the MESSY for Self-Report

Factor I. Appropriate Social Skill

(9)	I look at people when I talk to them	(0.49)
(10)	I have many friends	(0.36)
(12)	I help a friend who is hurt	(0.56)
(13)	I cheer up a friend who is sad	(0.57)
(16)	I feel happy when someone else does well	(0.46)
(20)	I tell people they look nice	(0.54)
(23)	I walk up to people and start a conversation	(0.36)
(24)	I say "thank you" and am happy when someone does something for me	(0.57)
(28)	I know how to make friends	(0.44)
(31)	I stick up for my friends	(0.43)
(32)	I look at people when they are speaking	(0.56)
(34)	I share what I have with others	(0.52)
(37)	I show my feelings	(0.46)
(40)	I take care of others' property as if it were my own	(0.38)
(42)	I call people by their names	(0.39)
(43)	I ask if I can be of help	(0.58)
(44)	I feel good if I help someone	(0.64)
(46)	I ask questions when talking with others	(0.42)
(50)	I feel sorry when I hurt someone	(0.50)
(52)	I join in games with other children	(0.37)
(55)	I do nice things for people who are nice to me	(0.59)
(56)	I ask others how they are, what they have been doing, etc.	(0.47)
(59)	I laugh at other people's jokes and funny stories	(0.42)

Eigenvalue = 10.59

Factor II. Inappropriate Assertiveness

(2)	I threaten people or act like a bully	(0.43)
(7)	I take or use things that are not mine without permission	(0.47)
(11)	I slap or hit when I am angry	(0.54)
(14)	I give other children dirty looks	(0.44)
(17)	I pick out other children's faults/mistakes	(0.35)
(19)	I break promises	(0.42)
(21)	I lie to get something I want	(0.53)
(22)	I pick on people to make them angry	(0.58)
(29)	I hurt others' feelings on purpose (I try to make people sad)	(0.52)
(30)	I make fun of others	(0.64)
(39)	I make sounds that bother others (burping, sniffing)	(0.50)
(41)	I speak too loudly	(0.36)
(53)	I get into fights a lot	(0.55)
(60)	I think that winning is everything	(0.33)
(61)	I hurt others when teasing them	(0.48)
(62)	I want to get even with someone who hurts me	(0.43)

Eigenvalue = 4.3

Factor III. Impulsive/recalcitrant

(3)	I become angry easily	(0.31)
(4)	I am bossy (tell people what to do instead of asking)	(0.46)
(5)	I gripe or complain often	(0.50)
(6)	I speak (break in) when someone else is speaking	(0.39)

(continued)

Table 2.1. First Order Varimax Loadings on the MESSY for Self-Report (continued)

(35) I am stubborn	(0.49)
Eigenvalue = 1.91	

Factor IV. Overconfident

(8) I brag about myself	(0.30)
(33) I think I know it all	(0.35)
(36) I act like I am better than other people	(0.35)
(57) I stay with others too long (wear out my welcome)	(0.52)
(58) I explain things more than I need to	(0.47)
Eigenvalue = 1.18	

Factor V. Jealousy/Withdrawal

(15) I feel angry or jealous when someone else does well	(0.50)
(38) I think people are picking on me when they are not	(0.43)
(49) I feel lonely	(0.46)
(54) I am jealous of other people	(0.48)
Eigenvalue = 1.09	

Miscellaneous Items

(1) I make other people laugh	(0.27)
(18) I always want to be first	(0.50)
(25) I like to be alone	(0.55)
(26) I am afraid to speak to people	(0.25)
(27) I keep secrets well	(0.13)
(45) I try to be better than everyone	(0.45)
(47) I see my friends often	(0.28)
(48) I play alone	(0.65)
(51) I like to be the leader	(0.61)

The number in parentheses on the left denotes where the item appears in the text presented to the child.

study of this type has been conducted with the MESSY (Matson et al., 1981). The investigators tested 58 children at an elementary laboratory school in Pittsburgh, Pennsylvania. The children ranged in age from 8 to 13 and were of superior intelligence. A number of measures, most of which will be reviewed later in this chapter, were included. Among these were role-played situations where direct observations were made of specific behaviors such as eye contact, number of words spoken, verbal content, facial expression and motor movements. The investigators also employed peer nominations, checklists including the MESSY, and structured interviews. Intelligence and gender significantly affected performance. Brighter children evinced more appropriate social behavior, while girls were both less aggressive and less assertive. Also, there was strong agreement between child and teacher evaluations of performance. In particular, peer nominations and teacher ratings were very

Table 2.2. First-Order Varimax Loadings on the MESSY for Teacher-Report

Factor I. Inappropriate Assertiveness/Impulsive

(2)	Threatens people or acts like a bully	(0.82)
(3)	Becomes angry easily	(0.80)
(4)	Is bossy (tells people what to do instead of asking)	(0.84)
(5)	Gripes or complains often	(0.85)
(6)	Speaks (break in) when someone else is speaking	(0.66)
(7)	Takes or uses things that are not his/hers without permission	(0.56)
(8)	Brags about himself/herself	(0.65)
(9)	Slaps or hits when angry	(0.83)
(11)	Gives other children dirty looks	(0.84)
(12)	Feels angry or jealous when someone else does well	(0.78)
(13)	Picks out other children's faults/mistakes	(0.79)
(14)	Always wants to be first	(0.65)
(15)	Breaks promises	(0.49)
(16)	Lies to get what he/she wants	(0.69)
(17)	Picks on people to make them angry	(0.87)
(21)	Hurts others' feelings on purpose (tries to make people sad)	(0.82)
(22)	Is a sore loser	(0.87)
(23)	Makes fun of others	(0.85)
(24)	Blames own problems	(0.78)
(27)	Thinks he/she knows it all	(0.75)
(29)	Is stubborn	(0.72)
(30)	Acts like he/she is better than others	(0.73)
(31)	Shows feelings	(0.55)
(32)	Thinks people are picking on him/her when they are not	(0.74)
(35)	Makes sounds that bother others (burping, sniffing)	(0.62)
(36)	Brags too much when he/she wins	(0.77)
(38)	Speaks too loudly	(0.68)
(42)	Defends self	(0.55)
(43)	Always thinks something bad is going to happen	(0.45)
(44)	Tries to be better than everyone	(0.67)
(48)	Gets upset when he/she has to wait for things	(0.62)
(49)	Likes to be the leader	(0.57)
(52)	Gets into fights a lot	(0.87)
(53)	Is jealous of other people	(0.84)
(55)	Tries to get others to do what he/she wants	(0.64)
(57)	Stays with others too long (wears out welcome)	(0.72)
(58)	Explains things more than needs to	(0.62)
(60)	Hurts others to get what he/she wants	(0.85)
(61)	Talks a lot about problems or worries	(0.57)
(62)	Thinks that winning is everything	(0.78)
(63)	Hurts others when teasing them	(0.82)
(64)	Wants to get even with someone who hurts him/her	(0.83)

Eigenvalue = 26.19

(Continued)

Table 2.2. First Order Varimax Loadings on the MESSY for Teacher-Report (continued)

Factor II. Appropriate Social Skills

(1)	Makes other people laugh (tells jokes, funny stories, etc.)	(0.35)
(10)	Helps a friend who is hurt	(0.69)
(18)	Walks up to people and starts a conversation	(0.63)
(19)	Says "thank you" and is happy when someone does something for him/her	(0.85)
(25)	Sticks up for friends	(0.72)
(26)	Looks at people when they are speaking	(0.69)
(28)	Smiles at people he/she knows	(0.67)
(33)	Thinks good things are going to happen	(0.54)
(34)	Works well on a team	(0.59)
(37)	Takes care of others' property as if it were his/her own	(0.44)
(39)	Calls people by their names	(0.64)
(40)	Asks if he/she can be of help	(0.75)
(41)	Feels good if he/she helps others	(0.66)
(45)	Asks questions when talking with others	(0.65)
(47)	Feels sorry when he/she hurts others	(0.51)
(50)	Joins in games with other children	(0.59)
(51)	Plays by the rules of a game	(0.44)
(54)	Does nice things for others who are nice to him/her	(0.72)
(56)	Asks others how they are, what they have been doing, etc.	(0.67)
(59)	Is friendly to new people he/she meets	(0.72)

Eigenvalue = 8.25

Miscellaneous Items

(20)	Is afraid to speak to people	(0.45)
(46)	Feels lonely	(0.40)

The number in parentheses on the left denotes where the item appears in the text presented to the rater.

positive. The measures that proved to be least correlated to the other tests were measures of role-play performance. Thus, at least when highly discrete measures of social behavior are used, it can be concluded that teacher reports on checklists such as the MESSY, MESSY self-report, and peer nominations are useful. However, it should also be noted that while peer nominations may be particularly sensitive to social dysfunction, they are in most cases impractical. This situation is the case since informed consent from all the children in the class would be required. Thus, checklists may be the most practical means of assessment.

Since these initial studies, a number of other experiments have been performed to extend these findings. In two such studies, data on deaf children were examined. Matson et al. (1985) evaluated 96 children from a state residential school for the deaf in Wisconsin. There were 58 males and 38 females, 8 to 19 years of age, averaging 14.8 years. Hearing was the primary handicap, but 12 children were mildly mentally retarded, 19 were learning disabled, and 1 was visually impaired. Teachers who filled out the scale had degrees in special (deaf) education with at least three years of experience. For the teacher report version there were two factors: inappropriate assertiveness/impulsiveness and appropriate social skills. The internal reliability of the scale was high, and in general the measure seemed workable and appropriate with this population.

It was also deemed appropriate to compare these social responses to emotional problems in this group of children. Thus, general measures of emotional problems with the AML Behavior Rating Scale (Cowen et al., 1973) and the Piers-Harris Self Concept Scale (Piers & Harris, 1964) were compared to social skills deficits. The 96 children described above were also studied. There were no differences by age or gender, but level of intelligence was a significant factor. More impaired children evinced additional problem behaviors. It was also the case that major deficit areas in social skills were closely related to major deficits in emotional problems as measured with the AML. These data are of considerable importance; they demonstrate that serious social deficits require careful assessment and remediation since they are often associated with a broad range of problem areas. However, interestingly at least with this group, self-concept problems and major social dysfunctions did not seem to be related.

Another comparison of social skills in deaf children was made between deaf and hearing impaired children (Macklin & Matson, 1985). There were 30 deaf and 30 normal hearing children matched in age and sex for comparison purposes. The scale was completed by each child's homeroom teacher. The hearing impaired children evinced more deficits in this area than the nonhandicapped group, with assertive responses being particularly lacking. Also, hearing impaired children were more likely to think others were picking on them. This research is important in that it clearly shows that social behavior can be adequately evaluated in hearing impaired persons.

Visually impaired children have also been systematically evaluated with the MESSY (Matson et al,. 1986). In the study, the authors tested 75 visually handicapped children and young adults ranging in age from 9 to 22 and averaging 14 years of age. All of these persons were attending programs for visually handicapped persons in northern and central Illinois with many eye conditions present including albinism, cataracts, optic atrophy, retinoblastomar, and degenerative myopia. Both self-report and teacher report information was obtained. To ensure accurate self-report information, a number of response modes were used with participants. In some cases the typical survey was employed in combination with a magnifying glass while in other instances large print using an IBM Orator Element was employed. For those persons who could not read print due to very severe visual impairments, cassette audiotapes of

ECSS—C

the scale were employed. Response alternatives also varied according to the individual student's communication method. Students using the printed survey form responded on the sheets. The other visually handicapped children and young adults responded on large-print answer sheets or with braille answer sheets.

The findings were in general very favorable. Interitem reliability was 93% for the teacher and 80% for the self-report. Similarly, high split half reliabilities were found. These results suggest the consistency of responses and the general workability of the MESSY with visually impaired children and young adults.

Other comparisons were also made primarily to evaluate the effect of visual impairment on social ability. This comparison showed that normally sighted children and youths performed better than the visually impaired sample. However, the degree of visual impairment did not seem to be of major importance. These data may suggest a threshold of visual acuity in relation to overall appropriate functioning. Another possible explanation is that interacting primarily with visually handicapped peers may inhibit proper functioning to some degree. An alternative solution may be to make greater efforts to mainstream these children where possible, or to make efforts to further specify where weaknesses in social functioning exist and to work on improving these responses.

It has also been shown that the social response evaluated on the MESSY may relate to a broad number of emotional problems. This was aptly demonstrated with deaf children (Matson et al., 1985). Furthermore, in a study by Kazdin et al. (1986), 262 children 62 girls and 200 boys, inpatients on a child psychiatry ward, were tested along with their mothers or maternal guardians. Among the DSM III diagnoses evinced by the children were conduct disorder (n=115), major depression (n=42), attention deficit disorder (n=26), adjustment disorder (n=18), anxiety disorder (n=12), psychosis (n=7), and other mental disorders (n=42). Children and parents and/or guardian were evaluated separately and within 7 to 10 days after admission to the unit. It was found that measures of increased helplessness were correlated with diminished social responsiveness as measured with the MESSY.

Another similarity between social skills and emotional functioning was reported by Helsel and Matson (1984). They evaluated 76 children from northern Illinois and found a strong relationship between social skills problems and depression in children, a relationship previously noted in adults (Lewinsohn, 1975). The problem areas were particularly strong with respect to social isolation and lack of assertiveness. It is therefore recommended that the professional working with depressed children should also consider employing measures of social skill to provide additional information on the extent of the problem and to target areas for psychologically and educationally based treatments.

An effort has been made to demonstrate the applicability of the MESSY for a range of subgroups in the general population of children. Mildly mentally retarded children, those of normal intelligence, visually impaired and hearing impaired persons have been tested. Also, while teachers have constituted the group of informant raters, parents and mental health workers should also be encouraged to use the scale. The items pertain more to specific behaviors than to particular settings such as the home or school. Therefore, the MESSY should have broad applicability.

Another measure of social skills with children designed specifically for school social problems — the TROSS-C — has recently been developed (Clark et al., 1985). These investigators had items which were selected from other rating scales, target behaviors that had been employed in empirically based studies of social skills, and social behaviors which have been shown to predict peer acceptance and/or popularity. The scale consists of 52 items which are filled out by the teacher. Items typical of the scale are: a) completes classroom assignments within required time; b) uses free time in an acceptable manner; c) interacts with peers; d) invites peers to play; e) displays sense of humor; f) invites peers to join an ongoing activity or group; and g) praises peers. Based on factor analysis, several subscales emerged: academic performance, social initiation, cooperation and peer reinforcement. The factors are descriptive and are geared toward the classroom. Concurrent validity has been established. The investigators conclude that the scale is a promising measure to screen social skills in children. As in the MESSY, a range of social/interpersonal behaviors can be evaluated. Also, it may be particularly good for classroom use.

In the initial study described above, normal I.Q. children were evaluated. Also, in a later effort, data on developmentally disabled children were evaluated (Gresham et al., 1986). The sample consisted of 250 mainstreamed school-age children from four different groups: a) behavior disordered, b) learning disabled, c)mildly mentally retarded, and d) nonhandicapped.

Ratings were completed by special education teachers who evaluated students in their class and same-sex, same-race, nonhandicapped peers. They factor analyzed their data, resulting in a replication of the factors found in this initial study. The samples consisted of 50% handicapped and 50% nonhandicapped persons. What these data suggest is that there do not seem to be great differences in social functioning between mildly handicapped and nonhandicapped children on this measure, at least for 1st to 8th graders. Of course, other explanations may be that the measure is not sufficiently sensitive or there were not sufficiently large numbers of handicapped children.

The development of the MESSY and the TROSS-C are important, since they were developed specifically for the evaluation of social interpersonal functioning of children. This development is recent, but even further developments in this area are critical as at least one criterion for the identification of social skills excesses and deficits and as a means of evaluating the effectiveness of various treatment programs designed to remediate this problem.

GENERAL MEASURES OF ADJUSTMENT

In addition to instruments that are specifically designed to assess social skills, measures have been developed as checklists which evaluate subcomponents of this problem. Also, they have as part of their overall evaluation a factor for social behavior. It would take a great deal of space to review all of these measures. Therefore, selective and popular instruments will be the focus of our brief review.

The two most popular of these measures in terms of empirical study are the Child Behavior Checklist and the Behavior Problem Checklist. Those measures are more typically thought of as general measures of child behavior. As such, they are often used in mental health clinics and when employed in the school setting are not geared specifically to school problems. The Louisville School Behavior Checklist is another general measure of psychopathology, with some implications for social behaviors in the school settings. As noted, there are also many other general measures. It would not be possible to review all of them here. Therefore, the reader is referred to Matson and Breuning (1983), Frame and Matson (1987), and Ollendick and Hersen (1984) for more detailed descriptions of this assessment literature.

Child Behavior Checklist.

This scale is one of the two most popular methods of evaluating overall psychopathology. There are self-rating, teacher-rating, and parent rating versions. Described by Achenbach and Edelbrock (1983), the Child Behavior Checklist is a 118 item checklist measure designed for children and youths between 4 to 18 years of age. This instrument is based on the concept that a taxonomic definition of adjustment problems is preferable. Thus, categories of psychological disorder are based on factor analyses. Among the areas which can be evaluated are depression, conduct disorder, hyperactivity, and social dysfunction. The social responses are of a very general nature but could be used as an initial means for screening for social dysfunction. Based on these data, a more specialized assessment using specific measures of social dysfunction could be used to identify specific areas of social skills deficits and excesses and the severity of various categories of disorder within the social performance area.

Behavior Problem Checklists.

As previously noted, the second most popular measure of overall functioning is the Behavior Problem Checklist (Quay & Peterson, 1975). This measure is the most extensively studied of all the child psychopathology measures. Walls et al., (1977), for example, found over 200 published and unpublished papers on the subject. And, like the Child Behavior Checklist, it has had areas of psychopathology defined on a factor analytic approach. A disadvantage of the Behavior Problem Checklist is that the categories are even more removed from generally accepted diagnosis as exemplified by DSM III when compared to the Child Behavior Checklist. Thus, it has not received general support beyond those persons who strongly advocate empirically defined diagnostic categories. Four major factors have typically emerged in research across a broad range of childhood populations such as institutionalized juvenile delinquents, regular school children, classrooms of emotionally disturbed children, clinic-referred children, and visually impaired persons. These categories include conduct disorder, personality problem, inadequacy-immaturity, and socialized delinquency. The conduct and inadequacy-immaturity factors are those most closely related to social skills problems. Once again, however, the factors are general and only a few items are specific to social skills.

We have briefly reviewed two separate measures of psychopathology that indirectly can be used to evaluate skills and should prove of interest as general screening measures for the educator or clinician. It would not be necessary to use one of these measures if one was fairly certain that social skills were the problem. However, it is also the case that many specific forms of psychopathology overlap with social skills excesses and deficits. We know this intuitively with conduct disorder and hyperactivity, and this assumption has been demonstrated empirically with childhood depression (Helsel & Matson, 1984). Thus, employing a general adjustment measure may be of benefit in developing a broad array of effective responses.

It should be cautioned that these general measures are not viewed as beneficial methods of identifying specific areas for psychological interventions or as a means of evaluating treatment outcome. They should instead be considered methods for screening. Identifying areas for treatment should include direct observation, role-playing, use of checklists specific to social skills such as on the MESSY, and, when applicable, peer nominations and ratings. These measures should be filled out where possible by the child, a parent or parents, and important others such as school teachers. Obviously, the idea is to ensure the highest possible levels of reliability and validity — not only for overall diagnostic areas such as social skills but in the *specific* areas where dysfunction is likely to be present. Whether the treatment or treatments being employed are behavioral, pharmacological, or otherwise, precise identification and description of the problem areas is of extreme importance. It is also true, however, that a comprehensive approach from broad to specific is an important concern in overall assessment. Therefore, a broad range of measures with different but overlapping areas of coverage is needed.

Direct Observation

Most social skills research to date has involved behavioral theories of assessment and treatment. The mainstay of behavioral assessment has been direct observation — an area which has taken on considerable importance in the area of social skills assessment. There is a long tradition for the use of these methods. Primarily, what is involved is the identification of discrete behaviors which are operationally defined. The responses must be observable; inferences dealing with mentalistic events are not typically part of the definition. This emphasis on observable behavior is due to low reliability of judges which comes from inability to identify unobservable characteristics of behavior. Based on current social skills methodology, behaviors that identified for assessment and treatment include eye contact, content of speech, number of words spoken, appropriateness of social affect, speech latency, voice volume, and overall assertiveness. These are typical responses and, in a sense, have been of considerable value for defining the concept of social skills.

Perhaps one of the most effective methods of assessment involves frequency counts of data in naturalistic settings. Typical of this procedure might be counting specific responses such as appropriate comments or insulting remarks made in the classroom. Of course these behaviors could be modified, or other responses might be substituted for these particular ones. Data might also be taken on the ward in a psychiatric hospital or in other, more naturalistic settings. In many respects it would be difficult to take data in the home, because parents might be involved in the interaction and parents may not have the skills to perform accurate assessments. Despite the advantages in terms of accuracy and the likely sensitivity to treatment change, this form of data collection is employed infrequently, mainly due to the expense. Trained staff may be required several hours a day. Also, rater reactivity can be problematic, that is, the presence of the rater can markedly affect the rate and type of responses children may display. Similarly, without taking a great deal of data it is likely that the information may not be representative of the child's typical performance. For these reasons, this form of direct observation has not become popular.

As noted, the implementation of direct observation in social skills training can be in any one of several environments. One of the most common has been analogue therapy sessions. The child would typically be evaluated by one or two adults, and four to six target behaviors would be reviewed based on responses to role-play scenes. Role-plays consist of components; a narrated description of a person who would be addressing the child in the context of the narrated situation; and, the child's response. A typical role-played scene would be as follows:

Narrator: You are out on the playground playing on one of the swings. Another child comes up to you and says:
    Role-Model Prompt: Get off that swing. I want to use it. You say . . .
    Child: _____

Based on the child's response, the identified target behaviors would be rated based on accuracy of performance.

The role-play assessment method has received attention for some time. It has been used in most of the studies both with children and adults who have been treated for social dysfunction. However, it should be cautioned that role-play assessment may have only limited reliability and validity, and the clinician should never use this method alone. Questioning of this method was first done by researchers working with adults, who found that role-play performance did not correlate with overt behavior in other social situations (Bellack et al., 1979; Bellack et al., 1978) — an issue that has more recently been addressed with children (Kazdin et al., 1984: For example, Kazdin et al. (1984) evaluated the social skills performance of 38 psychiatric inpatients who were 7 to 13 years of age. They completed measures to assess role-play performance, knowledge of social skills, self-efficacy and self-report social behaviors which were recorded for a number of diverse situations, along with direct observation in the hospital. Multiple measures of social behavior were also completed by staff, children, parents and teachers on the MESSY, Child Behavior Checklist, and Miller School Behavior Checklist. Role-play performance correlated significantly with child knowledge and self-efficacy but not with overt social behavior or self-report social behavior. While role-play assessments did not generally correlate with third-person measures, these third-party assessments did correlate with each other.

The major conclusion that can be drawn from these studies is that role-play assessments of social behavior may have limited generalizability to the natural environment. Another explanation is that these behaviors may encompass a much narrower range of performance than the general social skills measures, making them sensitive to only a very limited range of interpersonal responding. This latter point would also be of importance in making claims about the clinical significance or utility of social skills changes evaluated only via the role-play method. It may be that the role-play test is of limited utility as a means of observing and rating social functioning. However, based on these data it should not be concluded that role-plays are of no utility. Rather, is should be cautioned that this particular form of direct observation of social skills should not be used as the only means of evaluation. Also, it should be pointed out that this measure is probably the easiest and most convenient method of direct observation, and it is undoubtedly more sensitive to changes in actual behavior than checklists. Given the treatment sensitivity of the measure, it may prove to be useful as an indicator of initial change in social skills, but not as a means of evaluating long-term treatment outcome. Identifying initial change is important. However, few professional, direct-care staff, or parents are willing to wait many months for minimal signs of progress. This method may prove to be the easiest objective way of identifying whether a given social skills treatment should be terminated or continued in attempts to make long-term treatment changes.

Given some of the concerns with generalization of role-play responses to the natural environment and the recognized need for direct observation in the naturalistic setting, it is recommended that several of these assessment methods be used in combination. Thus, it will be our purpose to briefly review what we consider to be some of the major methods of role-play assessment.

Several role-play tests and methods have been developed. However, the standard approach is to either tailor situations specifically to a given child or to use a list of scenes that are based on common situations that children present. The scenes are presented to the child in a therapy room based on a description of the situation (narrator description), comment of the therapist taking the role of someone described in the narrated scene (role-model prompt), and the response of the child to the situation. The child is evaluated on discrete behaviors displayed during his/her answer, such as eye contact, voice volume, latency of speech, and content of speech. Specific feedback, prompts, and reinforcement for correct and incorrectly performed behaviors can then be provided. The behaviors listed in Table 2.3 are based on these specific responses. For children who have scenes designed specifically for them, comments of the child, relatives, the teacher, and, where applicable, professional staff are used to establish a set of situations. This method is often used, and it could be used in combination with standard lists of role-play scenes.

One of the first standardized lists of role-play scenes was that of Bornstein et al., (1977): the Behavioral Assertiveness Test for Children BAT-C. The assessment battery was comprised of nine interpersonal situations with which children were likely to present when experiencing social skills problems. A typical scene, which is administered in the fashion described, above would be:

Narrator: You're part of a small group in science class.
Your group is trying to come up with an idea for a project to present to the class. You start to give your idea when Amy begins to tell hers also.
Prompt: Hey, listen to my idea.

The BAT-C has been used in a number of studies with single case designs for determining level of deficiency and for determining treatment outcome (Van Hasselt et al., 1979). A 12-item revision of the BAT-C has been described by Ollendick and his colleagues (Ollendick, 1981;

A second measure of this type is described by Michelson et al. (1983) in their work at the University of Pittsburgh. As with other recently developed role-play assessments, there has been a move away from the more narrow assertiveness training to a broader social interpersonal context.

Perhaps the most extensively researched of the standardized role-play measures is the Social Skills Test for Children (SST-C) (Williamson et al., 1983). The researchers studied 104 children from second to sixth grades from laboratory schools in Baton Rouge, Louisiana. They established acceptable criterion validity in this study and social validity in another paper (Lethermon et al., 1982). In both instances a broad number of social skills scenes were employed, totaling 30. Among the topics covered in the scenes were giving praise, accepting praise, giving help, accepting help, and assertiveness. Typical of these scenes are the following

Accepting Help
Narrator: You're at recess, you fall down and hurt your leg. A friend says:
Role Model Prompt: Let me get the teacher.
Assertiveness:
Narrator: You brought a pencil to school and one of the boys breaks it. He laughs and says:
Role Model Prompt: Ha. Ha. I broke your pencil.
Accepting Help
Narrator You can't get your glue bottle open. A classmate notices and says:
Role-Model Prompt: Here, let me help you with that. Giving Help
Narrator: One of the girls is hurrying to get her things together to leave on her school bus. Her books fall everywhere. She says:
Role-Model Prompt: Oh, no! I'll miss my bus. I've gotta pick all this stuff up.

Stages that were followed in the development of the SST-C and are recommended to the reader in the development of their own social skill role-play scenes include: a) selection of role-play scenes (based on a conversation with child, teacher, and parents); and b) establishment of a procedure for administering the test and establishing a reliable scoring procedure.

These role-play procedures have proven to be useful, at least with some children. However, it should be kept in mind that this method is particularly vulnerable to faking by the child, or poor performance can result due to lack of motivation. However, unlike many assessment methods, this approach is fairly easy to carry out. It may provide additional information and, given that it is easy to conduct, it should be considered as a means of evaluating social skills excesses and deficits of children.

Direct observation is a very important dimension of assessing social skills excesses and deficits. It is highly recommended in one or both of the forms described here, using one of these variations or perhaps others. Certainly there are both advantages to this method and also some of the other methods we will review. The next method to be discussed is perhaps the method formally used for the longest period of time: sociometric ratings.

Sociometric Ratings

Evaluations of peers is another approach to the assessment of social skills in children, and it has received some attention. Researchers have suggested that these peer ratings might be particularly desirable in predicting later emotional difficulties (Cowen et al., 1973), although the validity of this assumption has been questioned more recently. It is also pointed out by La Greca (1981) that sociometric ratings may be too stable and general in item content to identify specific target behaviors for treatment or as a sensitive measure for evaluating treatment outcome. Similarly, they point out that sociometric ratings are often very time consuming to administer and score. Also, an important ethical/legal issue which recently has become a more prominent issue is that many school personnel are sensitive about having children rated and discussed in the presence of others, particularly given that the comments are being made by children rather than by professionals. It has also been our experience that if the child is being seen outside the school, such as in a mental health clinic, it is hard to get access to the school for these assessments. Furthermore, with inpatient settings there often is considerable turnover by children being evaluated and treated; this may result in failure to obtain a broad-based, school-oriented evaluation. Thus, it is difficult to get peer ratings simply because of lack of stability in the norm group. However, the stability and accuracy of this type of measure when optimal conditions are present should not be underrated, particularly given that correlations between some checklist measures of teachers and peer ratings may not always be high (La Greca, 1981).

One of the most common — if not the most common — form of sociometric evaluation is peer nomination. The most typically discussed peer nomination procedure was developed originally by Moreno (1953). With this method children are asked, either in the classroom or on the playground, to name those peers who are their best friends and/or with whom they would most like to play or work. In the case of elementary or secondary school children, the nominations are usually restricted to same-sex peers. A child's score is then computed as the number of nominations received. A variation of this method of preschoolers, which might also have applicability to older mentally retarded or other severely handicapped children, involves pictures of classmates mounted on a poster (McCandless & Marshall, 1957). Each child is then presented with the poster and asked to name all of the pictured children, followed by a request to point to the children with whom he or she would most like to play.

The methods listed above require only positive nominations. However, negative nominations have been added more recently (Dunnington, 1957; Moore & Updegraff, 1964). Thus, not only can highly favored children be identified, but from the standpoint of social skills training, those most in need of assistance can be readily identified. It should be pointed out, however, that only general categories of dysfunction can be identified. This initial screening would need to be followed up with efforts to specifically identify deficits and excesses using direct observations, checklists such as the MESSY, and role-play assessments.

A second method of sociometric evaluations is the peer rating procedure. With this method the child in a given group responds to questions such as how much would you like to play with a given child, using all classmates. Since all children are rated, more stable scores may be obtained. However, this approach is more time consuming and requires finer discriminations, given that all children are evaluated — distinction that may prove difficult for some children. Also, unlike peer nominations, a somewhat different concept may be tapped, with rankings such as likeability. The peer ratings procedure is also used with teachers, although less frequently. Those persons rated should also be considered, and other teacher data are likely to vary somewhat from that obtained from the children. If possible it would be good to obtain both types of information — the idea being that obtaining information from two sources would assist in obtaining a more comprehensive data base

A third type of sociometric method is the peer assessment procedure. With this method a series of key characteristics are listed and the child is provided with the opportunity to rate particular children on their similarity to particular characteristics. Two commonly employed methods that fit this general strategy are the Guess Who Technique (Hortshore et al., 1929) and the Bower Class Play Method (Bower, 1960). A series of behavioral descriptions are used in each of these instances, and classmates are asked to nominate their peers in response to these items. These and related procedures have been employed in research with normal I.Q. and mentally retarded children.

In addition to our review of peer nominations of social skills, it should be pointed out that more specialized methods also exist. Perhaps the best studied of these peer ratings deals with aggression (Walder et al., 1961). This more specialized topic is mentioned as of possible utility for sociometric ratings for a variety of subtopics or areas within social skills. This method is perhaps best used as a screening procedure to identify impaired children. However, given recent trends in confidentiality, having children rate other children may become less feasible. This is the case since parental consent of all children in the class is required.

Social Validation

A final assessment issue to consider is social validation. While not a formal assessment method, it is a useful procedure for applied work with children. The method can be used as a means of selecting targets for intervention and as a way to evaluate treatment outcome. The two major components of this procedure are social comparison and subjective evaluation (Kazdin & Matson, 1981).

Social comparison consists of observing others and using their behavior as a norm reference in establishing targets for intervention and for evaluating outcome. For example, Nutter and Reid (1978) were interested in training institutionalized, mentally retarded women to dress themselves and to select their own clothing in such a way as to coincide with current fashion. Developing appropriate skills in dressing fashionably represents an important focus because of its relevance to preparing persons for community life. The women were trained to coordinate the color combinations of their clothing. Before training, Nutter and Reid observed over 600 women in the community where the institutionalized residents would be likely to interact and included such settings as a shopping mall, a local restaurant, and a sidewalk. They observed persons of normal intelligence living in the community to assess the color combinations of clothing and the specific garments worn. The popular color combinations identified among persons served as the basis for training the mentally retarded residents. Training was designed to utilize prompts to teach the residents how to choose popular color combinations in clothes on a puzzle task. Actual appropriate dressing increased as a result of this training. At follow-up, conducted from 7 to 14 weeks later, the residents still maintained their skills in selecting color-coordinated clothing combinations.

Another approach is to have children rate specific behaviors and endorse which specific behaviors routinely employed in social skills training are of most import. Jackson and Brunder (1986) employed this method successfully with middle school children in Australia. Items were also rated by adults. It was found that children and adults endorsed similar items.

The sociometric method is an important and potentially useful method of rating social skills. As with the other approaches discussed, there are a number of strengths and liabilities with this method. Thus, multiple methods of assessment should be considered.

CONCLUSIONS

In this chapter a range of assessment options have been reviewed. It is recommended that the assessment procedures that are chosen be tailored to the individual child or at least to the particular setting where treatment is to occur. A number of assessment procedures and scenes have recently been developed. Thus, expansion of methods has been very rapid and is promising with respect to future developments in the evaluation of children's social skills. Also, it should be pointed out that various forms of assessment may have different advantages. Therefore, the educator or clinician should consider these various measurement devices and strategies in the context of which methods are likely to prove effective for a particular social skills problem with a particular child under particular conditions. Also, the purpose of the assessment should be considered. Are you trying to identify specific problem areas or are you trying to evaluate the effects of a given treatment? The issue being addressed may call for variations in the assessment procedures. Issues such as these should be of critical concern in making selection of assessment devices that are likely to lead to the best possible conclusion. These newer methods are tailored specifically to social skills for children. Given the great interest in the topic, it is highly likely that advancement in assessment will occur rapidly.

Chapter 3

Treatment Approaches

INTRODUCTION

In the preceding chapters, we have explored various definitions and ways of assessing social skills with children. We hope that the importance of excesses and deficits has been pointed out sufficiently to illustrate the importance of remediating behaviors in this broad category across a variety of children's handicaps and interpersonal difficulties. In general, the treatments for social skills are behaviourally based and theory bound. Therefore, it is less difficult to classify treatments for these remedial techniques than is the case for many other problems of children. This chapter will be organized around the major theoretical camps within the behavioral movement. They will include methods based on operant conditioning, social learning theory, and cognitive behaviour therapy. Each of the three theoretical issues followed by a review of some of the major theoretical issues followed by a description of specific studies which exemplify the particular approach.

From a historical point of view, the operant methods were the first found to be affective in treating social skills in children. The function of the earliest studies was to see if in fact such problems could be remediated. Once the improvement of skills in an analogue situation had been accomplished, more sophisticated and varied approaches to the problem were demonstrated to be effective for various client groups and in more naturalistic settings. It is important to note, however, that this research is in a newly emerging area and that much is likely to be done in the next few years. Thus, the techniques being described should not be viewed as static but rather as rapidly evolving ones. Social skills training of children is likely to be a major focus of child psychology and special education in the next decade, given the recognized importance and success of social skills training programs. A review of a few studies which exemplify the treatment techniques are presented. Thus, our discussion is not exhaustive but rather exemplifies current and past trends.

OPERANT CONDITIONING

Perhaps the most highly researched of the learning-based models of treatment is operant conditioning. The procedures — based on the research of B.F. Skinner (1953) in the animal laboratory, and many others in applied settings — are well documented. As the reader is likely aware of this history, it will not be covered here. Extensive coverage of the topic is, however, available elsewhere (Kazdin, 1978). The basic principles of operant conditioning involve the focus on overt observable and definable behavior, identifying antecedent and consequent events, and contingently applying reinforcement and punishment. In Table 3.1 a description of some of the major assets of this theoretical formulation are presented. It should be pointed out that a number of studies using this methodology have been employed with children. Many of the studies have been with very young children and have dealt with nonverbal behaviors such as play skills. A review of some sample studies will follow with our comments on issues to consider in implementation.

In one study the focus of treatment was increasing cooperative play of Martha, a 5-year-old preschooler (Hart et al., 1968). The child was in a class with 14 other children, and the focus was on integrating the child into more and better social reinforcers. Cooperative play via praise and

Table 3.1. Operant Conditioning Model: Factors Associated with Social Skills Treatment

Most frequently employs nonverbal behavior
Direct reinforcement of the behavior
Modeling, self-reinforcement, and role-playing are not used
Frequent use of tangible reinforcers
Often employed with children and the developmentally disabled
Performance under external control
Verbal communication is not typically required
Problem solving is not typically employed
Treatment is typically on a one to one basis
Treatment is often in the natural environment
Evaluation of treatment effects is typically done by numerical counts of operationally
    defined behaviours
Focus is on a few discrete behaviors

other social reinforcers. Coopertive play consisted of pulling a child or being pulled by a child in a wagon, handing an object to a child, or pouring into his hands or into a container held by him, helping a child by supporting him physically, or bringing, putting away or building houses etc, with building blocks or other toys, and sharing with others. Priming and shaping procedures were used since the target behaviors were not sufficiently in Martha's repertoire. These methods consisted of prompting the other children to speak to Martha or to initiate potentially cooperative situations with her (priming) and shaping by initially reinforcing all responsive verbalizations which the girl exhibited when in the general proximity of other children. This series of procedures proved to be very effective in enhancing appropriate play. The training program was very simplistic by today's standards. However, it was effective and obviously easy to implement. Many social problems are at least initially very mild. Thus, programs such as the one just described should be considered as a possible intervention strategy. And, with a few modifications such a program could be implemented in the home or in other social settings.

Another preschool study which exemplifies the operant approach is described by Reynolds and Risley (1968). They treated a 4-year-old girl in a preschool classroom of 15 children. Treatment centered on increasing verbalizations. This target behavior consisted of any speech from the child heard by the observers excluding responses which did not include words, such as shrieking, humming, or laughing. Treatment consisted of contingent attention toward the child by the teacher when the preschooler spoke. The form of the teacher's attention was evaluated according to the context of the child's verbalizations and the nature of the situation. However, whenever the child's verbalizations were in the form of a request for materials, the teacher would ask questions about the materials and how the child intended to use them. The materials would only be given contingent upon the child's responding to one or more such questions. Thus, if the child said that she wanted to paint, the teacher would praise her for saying what she wanted, and then ask her what she was going to paint or what other things she needed in order to paint. Again, she was praised for any verbal response that she made. The procedure was repeated several times and found to be highly effective.

Bryant and Budd (1984) describe an interesting program with five boys and one girl with mild academic and behavioral handicaps. These children ranged in age from 4 to 7 years of age. Treatment took place in an outpatient clinic of the University of Nebraska Medical Center. The training program was aimed at treating noncompliance, temper tantrums, inattentiveness, and social deficits in expressing needs to others,

ECSS—D

cooperative playing, and taking turns. Class was held for three hours, four mornings a week. Training sessions were conducted in a separate area of the classroom by the head teacher, using toys and materials found in the dramatic play/building activity area. First, children were provided with a rationale for the importance of sharing and how to share. Next, examples of appropriate sharing and playing were described and practiced by the children with the teacher's help and direction. Prompting, shaping, and social reinforcement were employed to ensure proper performance of the skills being trained. To enhance generalization of these skills, the teacher monitored the children during free play. When the skills training occured in these naturalistic settings, the teacher socially praised and reinforced these behaviors. Following training, sharing increased and negative interactions decreased markedly.

Operant methods have also been described as part of an overall classroom design. Filipczak et al. (1979) describe a comprehensive program of academic and social behaviors. Among the classroom work was a social skills training class. The subjects were junior high school students who evinced severe social and academic behaviors. The teachers assisted the students in learning skills for dealing with school, home, and community through a curriculum promoting appropriate interactions with school staff, parents, peers, and persons of authority pertinent to each setting. Emphasis was placed on teaching nonverbal behavior and small group interaction. Contingent management procedures were employed using both social and tangible reinforcers. The program was run over an entire school year.

It should be stressed that a particularly important aspect of this program was the combination of academic and social skills training. These response classes seem to be highly related particularly for junior and senior high students. Very high correlations in academic and social responses occur. Also, it is no accident that many of the studies we have described emphasize the teacher and classroom training. It is oftentimes desirable to consider the school and family as an important training setting for social skills problems of children. The traditional model of hourly clinic meetings is probably a less effective one. Emphasis should therefore be placed on training parents, teachers, and the children themselves for intervention in the naturalistic setting.

The reader will note a historical progression in the few examples described in this section on operant conditioning. A few discrete behaviors with a simple reinforcement program were described in the early research, moving to an emphasis on treating multiple collateral behaviors, involving parents with school-based programs, designing programs into specialized curriculums, and emphasizing academic as well as social behaviors, given the relationship between these responses. This trend continues and is exemplified by the final papers to be described in this section.

Recently, Kohler and Fowler (1985) discussed an interesting intervention with three girls, 5, 6, and 7 years of age. All the children were described as domineering and inconsiderate of other children. The purpose of the study was to increase prosocial behavior during free play activities. During these periods of time, all 14 children in the class had access to three or four different play materials rotated from a pool of 16 items. Materials used included building blocks, tinker toys, dominoes, and various board games. A classroom teacher was present throughout each session to monitor the children's noise level and to ensure appropriate use of the play materials. Specific target behaviors included invitations to play; child acceptance or refusal of play invitations; using social amenities such as "thank you," "I'm sorry," and "excuse me"; negative behaviors including derogatory remarks or uncomplimentary or rejecting statements and verbal directions which consisted of the child instructing or commanding another child to engage in a specific behavior.

Training consisted of emphasis on employing other children as training assistants. The trainer described and rehearsed invitations with classmates and each day appointed three children to direct an invitation to a target child during the free play phase. Children were selected on a volunteer basis, and the trainer nominated different children each day so that eventually all of the peers participated. The target child and all the children who assisted in treatment that day earned a colored sticker on the days they met predetermined criteria of appropriate interactions. Additionally, the entire group earned a reward when appropriate social play occured. This latter procedure is a very nice addition. In a classroom situation where intensive behavioral methods are used with a targeted child, a frequent concern of other children is why the problem child is receiving all the special attention and rewards. Thus, ensuring that *all* children exhibiting appropriate behavior are being reinforced is stressed. This procedure was used with all the target behaviors described in this study. These general treatment strategies would seem applicable for a variety of social interpersonal problems of children in a group format.

Another interesting, recent twist is described by Sainato et al. (1986). They also conducted a classroom training program — in this case with 16 children 4 to 6 years of age — for the three target children and their classmates. Four categories of social behavior were evaluated, including positive vocal-verbal responses, positive motor gestures such as hugging, touching with hand or hands, and waving. Reciprocal behaviors for both of these were also evident, including negative vocal-verbal behavior and negative motor gestures. The teachers monitored the play activities and offered ideas but generally did not prompt the children to engage in social interactions. The teacher announced that she had a new helper and then asked the child to come to the front of the class. The teacher awarded the child a large "manager" button to wear for the next two weeks. His job consisted of leading and/or directing the class in previously rated, highly preferred activities which included directing the feeding of the class guinea pig, collecting milk money and taking lunch count, ringing the bell for clean-up time, and handing out the keys to the barber shop and shoe stores. Prior to beginning school each day, the teacher reviewed the manager's duties with the target child and the rest of the class. In addition, a picture board dipicting the manager's major tasks was displayed in front of the classroom to prompt the target child not to forget an assignment. The child placed in the manager's role resulted in dramatic improvement in social interactions.

In this section an effort has been made to describe examples of the operant approach to social skills training. As noted, a progression in the type and format of social skills training is apparent. Initial studies involved only one or two discrete behaviors via direct reinforcement by an adult, usually the parent or teacher. This focus has shifted to take into account multiple collateral behaviors and involving classmates and siblings in the treatment. These later methods have been necessitated by the lack of generalization of more focused treatments and the realization that the entire ecosystem in which the child lives must be considered if the most effective treatment is to be provided. Thus, the social learning and cognitive behavior therapy methods were considered to further enhance treatment of social problems in children.

The cognitive and social learning procedures are perhaps the most extensively studied of the methods with children in the last few years. For our review this section of the chapter will be divided into cognitive and social learning in that order. Once again, the review will not be exhaustive but will exemplify the major treatment approaches.

COGNITIVE BEHAVIOR THERAPY

The cognitive behavioral approach is a loosely defined group of procedures which take into account more specifically internal events, primarily cognition. The notion is that these covert activities can be tapped in ways to enhance learning. Particular emphasis is placed on the child's active participation and the training of self-therapy via decision making, self-reinforcement, and other self-regulation strategies.

In Table 3.2 we present a series of factors which fall in this general category of treatment.

One of the primary models of cognitive behavioral training is called social problem solving (Shure, Spivack, & Jaeger, 1971). The assumptions of this approach are that cognitive-interpersonal problem-solving skills can be learned and that such skills bear directly on improved adjustment in social behavior. An emphasis of this approach is on teaching problem-solving skills. The procedures are typically used with small children and are employed by the teacher via a structured curriculum (see Chapter 4 on curriculum). The program consists of a series of brief, primary, verbal daily games involving small groups of four to six children. The earliest games deal with the understanding of some specifically selected verbal skills thought to be related to alternative, consequential, and causal thinking. Language concepts are emphasized. Each new step is built directly on preceding ones and the program continues with training "if-then" logic as well as in the identification of emotions in others. Some researchers have suggested that there appear to be stable, consistent relationships between these problem-solving skills and inependently observed behavior (Rickel et al., 1983). This model does diverge from other methods in that general principles are being taught rather than discrete skills. The idea is that by following this procedure generalization of appropriate responding may be enhanced. This procedure is followed in a systematic, step-by-step process.

The first aspect of this model involves problem definition and formulation. One way this is accomplished is by compiling problem situations and then discussing the situations with the child. This review helps the child understand the various social problems he or she is likely to encounter. A variety of problems may be presented to help the child

Table 3.2. Cognitive Behavior Therapy Model: Factors Associated with
Social Skills Treatment

Most frequently employs verbal/interpersonal responses
Self-reinforcement, social reinforcement, and vicarious reinforcement are common
Direct reinforcement is typically not used
Modeling and role-playing are often used
Tangible reinforcement are typically not used
Employed with adults and in a few cases children and the mildly handicapped
Performed largely under internal control
Verbal communication is required
Problem solving is often employed
Treatment is typically on a one-to-one basis
Evaluation of treatment effects is typically done by numerical counts of operationally
    defined behaviors with checklists and other measures
Focus is on several discrete behaviors

better understand and consolidate this view. Among the techniques employed are the identification of feelings and the behaviors that can produce these feelings. A second important aspect of this cognitive educational approach is determining alternatives to the problematic social behaviors. Once again, a teaching approach with lectures and pictorial presentations is emphasized. Children might be asked to participate by listing alternatives themselves as well as those presented by the teacher. A third step is predicting consequences. Discussions and examples of how one's behavior affects others are reviewed. Finally, the child with the instructor's assistance evaluates the new behavior that has been performed. As with problem identification, the child may need guidance and assistance in how well he or she is performing these new skills.

Some cautionary notes should be made on this particular procedure. It should be emphasized that this method would likely work better with older children and those without developmental disabilities such as mental retardation and learning disabilities. Similarly, these methods are geared primarily toward a classroom setting with children who are highly motivated. As with other treatment methods to be discussed in this chapter, there are most certainly a number of positives. There should be a variety of alternatives available so that the best fit between the child and a given social skills training approach can be provided.

Another interesting cognitive behavioral method involves self-instruction. One variation of this method is described by Fisher and Wollersheim (1986). They employed classroom tutors. Training included short discussions about topics of interest about pets, friends at school, and other interests. Also, the tutors were strongly encouraged to engage in as many "friendly" behaviors as possible with the children. Specific behaviors were reinforced, including eye contact, verbal reinforcement, head orientation, position facial expression, and pleasantness of vocal expressions. Children were taught how to reinforce their own behavior along the lines described above, as well as how to reinforce oneself for correct responses.

The programs described above largely emphasize classroom instruction. It should be stressed that clinical settings — such as mental health clinics, centers, and institutions — and the home may also prove useful for treatment. And, some authors have described cognitive behavioral treatment programs in these environments. It should be emphasized that self-control strategies are one of the more highly emphasized of the cognitive strategies. Rehm (1977) focused on increasing rates of self-rewarding behaviors and/or decreasing rates of self-punitive behaviors. Specific procedures involve both direct contingency manipulation, and skills training in self-reinforcement. The emphasis in this approach is on the treatment of covert processes as behaviors. These events are considered operants which can be modified with reinforcement and punishment in much the same way as observable behavior.

The treatment program involves specific training in self-monitoring, behavioral rehearsal, role playing, and conducting functional analyses outside of the treatment setting. This task is generally accomplished in a one-to-one therapist client meeting in a therapy room. With small children, puppets and toys may serve as a medium in which to frame the learning task. For example, the therapist and child may role-play a social interaction with puppets. Also, homework assignments, review of past events, and discussions of how to deal with awkward social situations are integral aspects of the program. This method is perhaps best applied with adolesents. However, as a general rule of thumb, smaller children when treated with these methods will require greater support. Support should include family training in a client setting and via parent work with the child at home.

In one interesting study Billings and Wasik (1985) used cognitive behavioral methods with children in a Head Start center in rural North Carolina. The children were 4 years of age and from low-income families. Behaviors focused on were academic off-task, disruptive behavior, inattention, and a general category referred to as undesirable behavior. A self-instruction training program was implemented. This treatment involved modeling the task while talking aloud, having the child perform the task while the trainer instructed aloud, and having the child perform the task talking aloud to himself while the trainer whispered softly. The child was then asked to perform the task whispering softly while the trainer made lip movements but no sounds. Next, the child performed the task making lip movements without sound while the trainer covertly assisted. Then, the child performed the skill with covert self-instructions. When the sequence described above was completed, the trainer returned to step one and repeated this procedure with another task.

In this study, previous efforts of Bornstein and Quevillon (1976) were replicated using a method based on Meichenbaum and Goodman (1971), who used modeling, overt and covert rehearsal, prompts, feedback, and social reinforcement to train hyperactive children by having them think before they act. Bornstein (1985) argues that these methods are very effective. He also has some comments about where this procedure is likely to go as on effective treatment. Person variables are perhaps the most salient of these factors for the clinician to consider. Issues such as whether the person is more controlled by internal versus external variables is of obvious interest with children receiving instructional training. Motivational factors are a broader but related issue. It is hoped that researchers will be able to assist in answering these clinical issues. Past research tells us, however, that such person variables are difficult to isolate in child treatment.

A final example method to be discussed in cognitive behavior therapy is the social problem-solving method (Christoff et al., 1985). They treated four girls and two boys, 12 to 14 years of age. Children were referred from school based on a lack of effective socialization with peers. Other difficulties among these students were having few friends and being identified by school staff as being loners. The first phase of treatment involved four problem-solving skills training sessions. Initially, the therapist offered a rationale for acquiring problem-solving skills, outlining components of effective problem-solving. The group was then trained in applying the skills of an interpersonal problem situation. During the remaining sessions, the therapists reviewed the components of problem-solving and involved the group in verbalizing how they would apply the skills to a range of other interpersonal problems. As part of the session, students completed a work sheet on which they applied the skills to an interpersonal problem of their choice and discussed it during the subsequent session. The aspects of a problem-solving practiced in the sessions were a) recognizing a situation as a problem, b) defining the problem completely, c) generating multiple solutions, c) evaluating the probable negative and positive consequences of each solution, d) determining the best solution, and e) developing a plan for implementing the solution. The procedure just described was used for tasks such as joining a group conversation, initiating a conversation with a peer, requesting a peer to engage in a mutual activity, and making a request of an adult.

For the next four sessions, social skills training was conducted. Topics varied across sessions and were related to improving conversational skills. Topics included listening skills, talking about oneself, initiating conversations, and making requests of others. Students role-played skills with one another and were given feedback by the therapists and other group members on their performance. At the end of each session students were assigned homework to practice the skills trained that day. The effects were very dramatic and in a positive direction.

Several cognitively based interventions can be employed. The techniques we have described above are based on the notion that behavior is influenced by processes such as perceptions, thoughts, beliefs, images, and self-statements (referred to earlier in this section as self-instructions). Perceptions, which have not been a focus of social skills treatment with children, are most certainly an area for future concern. For example, a person who believes that people are friendly may initiate social responses such as greetings. The belief (cognitive process) leads to greeting and chatting with others, which in turn generates positive consequences for that person such as social reinforcement and other positive social consequences from others.

Cognitive development is a key issue in this approach — perhaps more so than for the other two approaches (operant conditioning and social learning theory). Cognitive behavior therapy seems to have great potential for cutting down the amount of therapist time, since the child at least in part becomes his or her own therapist. And, because the child has control over these special skills, generalization and maintenance are particularly promising. Conversely, a certain level of cognitive ability and motivation above the other two approaches is probably necessary. One method of promoting the internal control is initial emphasis on external events. Hopefully, with correct performance external reinforcers become internalized (Kazdin, 1984). Along these same lines and in an attempt to promote generalizatiom, molar versus molecular skills are emphasized. Thus, learning problem solving and other general strategies are prominent features of treatment. Such an approach is not always easy or practical, however. Therefore, a variety of methods are suggested. The final of the three global methods to be reviewed is social learning theory.

SOCIAL LEARNING THEORY

The social learning approach puts particular emphasis on modeling and role playing. The assumption is that social skills can be improved markedly by observing and practicing various social interpersonal behaviors. One aspect of this technique is the notion that a skill deficiency exists. This may not always be the case as pointed out in the assessment chapter. Therefore, a careful and thorough assessment ensuring that maximal motivation is present is essential in selecting a treatment. For the child who has the prerequisite skill, operant methods in the form of social and/or tangible reinforcers are sufficient. In the case of a recognized skill deficit, social skills training based on modeling is a likely alternative.

Social learning theory methods are aptly described in Table 3.3. As with the other two major approaches to treatment, a review of important components in the training is provided. One aspect of training is the emphasis on self and social reinforcers. And, while tangible reinforcers are sometimes needed, the emphasis on the latter categories of reinforcement are important since they can be generalized easily to the natural environment. Also, we know that modeling and role-playing

Table 3.3. Social Learning Theory Model: Factors Associated with Social Skills Treatment

Most frequently employs verbal/interpersonal responses
Social reinforcement and vicarious reinforcement are as common as direct reinforcement
Modeling and role-playing are commonly used
Self-reinforcement is not used
Tangible reinforcers are used sometimes
Employed with adults, older children, and mildly handicapped (e.g., mentally retarded)
    persons
Performed under external control
Verbal communication is required
Problem solving is typically employed
Treatment is conducted on a one-to-one basis and also in groups
Evaluation of treatment effects is typically done by numerical counts of operationally
    defined behaviors with checklists and other measures
Focus is on several discrete behaviors

can be powerful learning strategies. Their use in this particular approach is more structured and more heavily emphasized than with the other two major theoretical formulations and is the basis for the social learning method.

The basis of the social learning approach has been established in the laboratory and has been tested extensively with schizophrenics (Hersen & Bellack, 1976) and mentally retarded adults (Senatore et al., 1982: Matson & Zeiss, 1979). Following the work of McFall and Lillesand (1971) with college students evincing poor assertiveness skills, the authors noted above developed a standard set of training procedures. A study by Matson et al. (1980) typfiles the methods. They treated four children who were inpatients in the psychiatry department of the University of Pittsburgh School of Medicine. There were two boys and two girls: three 11-year-olds and one 9-year-old. All the children had great trouble in adapting at home and at school. Two of the children were in the dull normal range of intelligence, while the other two were of normal intelligence.

Training was oriented around social skills scenerios devised for these children based on typical problems that they exhibited. Each scene was broken into three parts; narrator, role-model prompt, and the client's response. Here is an example:

Narrator (Therapist): Imagine that a friend has just completed a very hard puzzle. She comes over to you and says . . .
Role-Model Prompter (serving as the model): *(Walks over with puzzle)* Look, (name of child), I have finished my puzzle. *(Followed by subject's response.)*

The narrator stood to the side of the room and described the situation;

then the role-model prompter and subject acted out the scene. The assessment was conducted in the training room by raters in an adjoining observation room through a one-way mirror. Separate training of appropriate verbal responses were: appropriate verbal content such as giving compliments, giving help, and making appropriate requests; appropriate affect, which included subcategories including voice pitch, volume, and facial mannerisms. A third behavior treated was appropriate eye contact. The facial response category was appropriate body posture, which focused primarily on sitting quietly.

The social skills training format described above is typically implemented on an individual basis. However, in this particular case a group format was used. One child who performed a particular skill well would be asked to act out a role-play scene (this approach allows for the use of other sides as models rather than adults). Using 3 × 5 index cards with scenes written on them, the narrator-trainer read the information from the card and attempted to elicit a response from the child who was participating in the role-play. Based on the quality of the child's response to the role-model prompter's statement, the narrator would then either re-present the same scene and demonstrate appropriate responding or present and narrate the next scene in the sequence. Training involved instructions, information feedback, modeling, role-playing, and social reinforcement on verbal behavior, body posture, affect, and eye contact. Treatment rotated from child to child. Thus, active participation was paired with observational learning in a system that proved to be very effective.

The range of methods in the social learning approach is less varied than with the operant conditioning and cognitive behavior therapy methods. The technique has been a popular one and is perhaps used most with children 10 years of age and above. And, as discussed later in this book, this method has been effectively used with mentally retarded children (Matson et al., 1980). As a response to criticism one very useful approach to treatment has been to focus, where possible, on training the family unit. Such an approach is important since the carryover (generalization) of desired responses is greatly increased. Typical of this social learning approach to social skills training is the training model of Serna et al. (1986). These researchers worked on a number of interaction skills, including giving and accepting criticism and giving and following instructions. Within these global constructs a series of very specific behaviors were trained. For example, parents were taught to do the following when giving instructions: a) face the person; b) maintain eye contact; c) keep a neutral facial expression; d) keep a straight posture; e) get the youth's attention by calling his/her name; f) state the instruction in the form of a request, being specific about the required behavior;

g) give a rationale for the request; h) ask the adolescent if (s)he understands; i) explain further the instructions if the adolescent did not understand them; j) ask him or her to perform the desired task; and k) when the adolescent agreed to follow the instructions by asking the adult to state a positive consequence for following the instructions. In addition to teaching a sequence of responses to a general goal, various nonverbal behaviors were trained including appropriate eye contact, facial expression, body posture, and head nods.

Skills training sessions were held separately for the seven adolescents aged 13 to 17, for the five adolescents aged 14 to 18, and for the parents, who were also worked with in groups. While the number of persons in each group was not specified our experience has been that with two leaders, groups of four to eight persons can be adequately trained. Training procedures such as those described in the Matson et al. (1980) paper were employed. These strategies include role-playing, modeling, instructions, feedback, and social reinforcers. Additionally, and for the parent group, some specific instructional components were included. These were a) a trouble-shooting component for the discussion of successful and unsuccessful parent-youth interactions in the home during the previous week; b) a rationale component for encouraging the parents to learn new parenting behaviors to build a positive and reciprocal parent-adolescent relationship; and, c) an information component for providing the parents with information about adolescent growth, simple behavioral techniques and their effects, and adolescent social behaviors concerning peers groups, and authority figures that related to recent parent-youth problems. This program proved effective and was an ambitious and more comprehensive program than what was described in the previous social learning study. Where possible, the clinician should include parents and siblings and should focus on a range of target behaviors. However, such a focus is not always possible, in those cases a program such as the approach of Matson et al. (1980) should be considered.

When using social learning programs various options for effective operant-based methods of teaching social skills can and should be considered as well. One interesting possibility is the program of Pravder and Israel (1983). They treated four boys and two girls who lived at a treatment-oriented group home for behaviorally disordered children. Three of the children did not attend public school due to problems with their behavior. When the social skills program described here was started a token economy program in the home was in effect. This strategy is significant, since we now believe that training in naturalistic settings is very important to ensure the most effective treatment and that the more naturalistic the setting in which treatment is provided, the more powerful the treatment is likely to be (Ollendick & Cerny, 1981).

Training was carried out in a simulated group home five evenings per week. Daily activities consisted of two 15-minute sessions separated by a 10-minute break. During the sessions the children worked on their regular school homework. The emphasis in the program was the move from an adult-monitored, peer-managed contingency system to a completely peer-administered system and finally the withdrawal of the system and a transition from an adult-administered group contingency system to the withdrawal of the system. This goal was accomplished in stages. First, a group contingency was used. This procedure consisted of having the tutor responsible for the group contingency period explain that the entire class could receive up to 10 points for on-task behavior engaged in by the entire group. At the end of the session, points (a form of tokens) were dispensed to the children for doing their homework and for refraining from speaking without permission. Points could be traded in for special activities and snacks. Also, the tutor gave the children feedback at the end of the period including praise for on-task behavior and information on how to receive more points on the following day.

A second phase involved the tutor training the children in the skills necessary to be appropriate helpers. The children were taught to ignore inappropriate behavior and praise on-task behavior. Both the content and affect associated with praise were modeled by the tutor and role-played by the children. Procedures for implementing the peer-administered treatment were explained to the children, followed by role-playing with instructions, performance feedback, and social reinforcement. Beginning each session, the children received pieces of paper with their names on it and the name of another randomly selected child. The individual receiving the paper was designated as the helper, and the assigned child was to be the buddy or special playmate for the day. The designated child was to do his or her homework and to monitor the target child's performance. Following the session, the helper dispensed from 0 to 5 points to the target child, with no points being given for off-task behavior occured during the entire session.

During the classroom break period after training, the tutor met with each pair individually so that the helper could inform the monitored child of points earned. Feedback included praise for appropriate behavior and ideas concerning how to earn more points the following day. The tutor assisted the helpers if they had difficulty giving clear feedback. The target child then left the room and the tutor informed the helper of whether the tutor's evaluation of the target was accurate. If they both allotted the same number of points to the target, the helper received three points. If there was a point difference, the helper received two points. No points were dispensed to the helper if the discrepancy was greater than one point. The helper could also receive two points for giving the targeted child appropriate feedback. Various strategies were also used to fade out the tutor. The basic concept was to decrease instructions, role-playing, and related behavioral procedures as the child's behavior improved. This phase is a very important one which is often overlooked. The systematic removal of treatment or perhaps more accurately shifting the focus of control and responsibility from adults or other children to the afflicted person should be a major focus of treatment.

SUMMARY

In this chapter we reviewed some of the advances made in the treatment of social skills problems in children. The interventions described pertain to the work of psychologists in the main. However, educators and psychologists have worked with various developmentally disabled groups and in the design of curriculum that can be employed in the classroom. These treatment efforts will be discussed at length in the chapters to follow.

A review of the social skills training literature points to several interesting and striking developments in the field. From the inception of applied behavior analysis, social skills training of children has been a focus of study. The early studies in the field typically dealt with reinforcing single response with concrete or social reinforcers for very limited time periods. The major function that studies of this type served were to demonstrate that rudimentary behaviors of this type could be modified. The focus has changed considerably since the time when treatment emphasized parent and peer involvement, internal states and self-management, and training that lasted for substantial portions of the day. The current trend toward attempts will likely continue, given the success of social skills training programs and the growing recognition of their importance.

Chapter 4

Developing and Implementing a Social Skills Curriculum with Children

INTRODUCTION

In this chapter, we shall discuss briefly issues related to the development and implementation of a social skills curriculum for children. Additionally, we will present an outline of the 12-week curriculum used by Ollendick in his social competency project (Ollendick, 1982). As noted in earlier chapters, there are many different ways to conduct social skills training. In general, these treatment approaches are based on the principles of operant conditioning, social learning theory, and cognitive behavior therapy. Here, we describe a cognitive — social learning approach (please see Chapter 3 on Treatment Approaches for a review of other procedures which fall into this topic) which borrows heavily from these various perspectives.

In developing a social skills curriculum for children, there are several issues to consider. Among them are factors related to the characteristics of the children selected for treatment and the nature of the precise social skill deficits that they exhibit, the content and process of the training procedure itself and how best to evaluate the success of the program. Although these factors may seem obvious to the discerning reader, there are many instances in the research literature and in clinical practice where standard "packages" are applied and where these factors are seemingly ignored. Social skills training, like other treatment procedures, needs to be tailored to specific individuals who function in particular settings with particular problems. There is no "one way" to do social skills training, as we have elaborated on earlier in this text. Let us explore these issues briefly prior to proceeding to a description of one representative treatment protocol.

First, it should be obvious that the content and the process of social skills training may need to differ for children, who vary in age and presenting problems. Young preschool children may benefit maximally from a direct teaching approach in which specific behaviors are identified and reinforced. However, less of a gain may occur from a cognitive approach in which verbal self-instruction and self-control strategies are used. As noted by Higa et al. (1979), children below 6 years of age may profit less from self-instructional training, since attending to both self-instructions *and* task performance is distracting and confusing to the child. Older children and adolescents (above 6 years), however, seem to improve performance with the addition of self-instruction. These findings, along with other developmental research, suggest that self-instructional training and other cognitive-based procedures are better suited for children who possess sufficient cognitive skills to benefit from their use (Ollendick & Cerny, 1981). Although untested at this time, an extension of these findings to the severely developmentally delayed would likely require similar precautions. Thus, characteristics of the children such as their developmental level are important in the selection of specific intervention strategies that might lead to significant behavior change.

Similarly, the content of the training program should address specific skill deficits at specific age levels. Such behaviors as cooperating and taking turns, starting up a conversation, and entering a group take on different expressions according to the developmental level of the child. Although clear developmental norms are not available, young children are rarely seen introducing themselves when entering a group. Typically, they simply approach the group and ask (if not demand) to play. In contrast, older children and adolescents typically extend greetings, introduce themselves, and *then* ask to participate. It is evident that we are sorely in need of firm developmental markers for the many social behaviors trained in social skills programs. Young children are not adolescents, let alone young adults. Oftentimes it appears as if we are training such youngsters to be miniature "grownups".

In a related vein, we must begin to develop greater awareness of the specific social problems exhibited by the children with whom we work. To some extent, such differences are reflected in different diagnostic groupings. Socially withdrawn and inhibited children are known to approach a group in a cautious, timid manner — described as "hovering" by Putallaz and Gottman (1981), Gottman et al. (1975), and Francis and Ollendick (in press). Aggressive children are observed to force themselves on the group, frequently altering the course of action by making themselves the center of attention. Still, autistic children may be oblivious to the group, seemingly unaware of its presence. Surely, such children require not only different approaches to intervention, but also require the acquisition of a set of behaviors that vary closely with their developmental level and diagnostic status.

Related to issues of the process and content of training are a set of evaluative issues. In Chapter 2, we described a set of assessment strategies that have proven useful in the identification and evaluation of skill-deficient children. A note of caution is in order, however. Age related verbal and cognitive abilities directly affect the appropriateness of certain methods of assessment (Ollendick & Hersen, 1984). Self-monitoring, for instance, requires the ability to compare one's own performance against a standard and to accurately judge occurrence or nonoccurrence of targeted events and behaviors. Young children (as noted earlier) may lack the requisite ability to self-monitor, and such procedures might be better used with older children. Age related variables also place constraints on the use of certain self-report, role-play, and sociometric measures. For example, it has been noted that sociometric devices need to be simplified and presented in pictorial form to young children. There are interesting adaptions to assessment procedures which may prove helpful. The picture sociometric for example, provides the child with a set of concrete, visual cues regarding the child to be rated, and, of course, the child is not required to read the names of those being rated. The roster-and-rating method, frequently used with older children, is simply not appropriate for younger children. Similarly, many self-reports of social skills such as assertion (Deluty, 1979; Michelson & Wood, 1982; Ollendick, 1984; Scanlon & Ollendick, 1985) will not be appropriate for children under about 8 years of age.

Other methods of assessment are not without their own age-related constraints. Although untested at this time, it seems plausible that reactivity to behavorial observation may also be age related. For example, the social comparison literature suggests that as children become older, they compare and evaluate their own behavior more directly against relevant social norms (see, e.g., Ruple et al., 1976). While an adults's presence might not serve as a cue for such an evaluation with younger children, or for that matter with adolescents, it might do so for the middle-age child. Confirmation of this possibility awaits empirical evaluation, however.

In brief, there are a number of issues that need to be considered when developing a social skills curriculum. Probably the most important of these is the child's ever-changing developmental status. Behaviors that are appropriate at one age may be less so earlier or later. This fact may also apply with treatment procedures. We obviously need to keep these developmental considerations in mind as we design our intervention strategies and attempt to evaluate them.

In the following section we shall illustrate a social skills curriculum for 8- to 10-year-old children who evince socially withdrawn or aggressive behavior.

COGNITIVE BEHAVIORAL CURRICULUM

This particular protocol was designed specifically for children who displayed deficits or excesses in carrying on a conversation, entering a group, cooperating with others, and being assertive in social situations. In this latter area, they showed deficits in standing up for their own rights, refusing unreasonable requests, making their own decisions, and giving as well as receiving positive compliments. In addition, these children were deficient in affect recognition skills and role-taking skills. More specifically, they seemed unable to take the role or assume the perspective of other children. As noted by several investigators (e.g., Dodge, 1980; Nasby et al., 1980; Rule et al., 1974), such deficiencies have been associated with the misperception of social events and the misattribution of intent (especially hostile intent).

The children were treated in small groups of six to nine children. A group typically was comprised of two or three aggressive children, two or three withdrawn children, or two or three popular children. The popular children were included to provide role-models for the "dysfunctional" children. In this instance, the children were assessed on teacher ratings, sociometric ratings, behavioral observations, and select self-report measures. A cognitive behavioral approach, based on the work of Meichenbaum (1977), Ollendick and Hersen (1979) and Spivack and Shure (1974) was used. Essentially, behavioral skills training (instruction, modeling, role-playing, and reinforcement) was combined with verbal self-instruction and social problem-solving strategies. Although a systematic comparison of this integrated approach to other procedures or to a control group was not undertaken, it was found to produce clear changes in these children following training. Children improved in sociometric status and overt social behavior, and on self-reports of assertiveness and locus-of-control. A systematic evaluation of the procedures is currently under way. An outline of the curriculum follows.

A Cognitive-Behavioral Training Protocol for Aggressive and
Withdrawn Children.

Session 1

Objectives: 1) Introduce group members
                         2) Provide a rationale for program and for child-
                            ren's participation in the program
                         3) Provide overview of program's goals, duration,
                            etc.
                         4) Establish ground rules
                         5) Introduce "thinking aloud," role-playing, and
                            general group format

Activities: 1) "What comes next?" game
                         2) Homework completion chart
                         3) Craft activity: write rules on construction paper
                         4) Homework # 1

Materials: 1) Homework booklet
                         2) Homework chart
                         3) Construction paper
                         4) Magic markers
                         5) Thinking aloud cards
                         6) Stickers

Procedure: The therapist initiates discussion of the rationale for the
group. He or she might say something like: "This is a group to help you
learn ways of getting along with other people. You'll learn things like
how to meet people, make friends, and deal with "tough" situations
with friends, parents, and teachers. For example, some people feel shy
or embarrassed when they meet new people. Does that ever happen to
any of you? (Solicit children's response here.) When is it hard for you to
get along with people? (Children respond.) When is it easy for you to get
along with people? (Children respond.)" The therapist should encour-
age response to this topic by *all* group members in order to delineate
specific problem areas. Following this, the therapist begins discussion of
the group process, noting the following points: a) the group will meet
once a week for 12 weeks; b) activities will include working on projects,
playing games, acting things out, and listening to themselves on tape
recorders; and c) that homework will be assigned after each group, and
will be reviewed at the beginning of the next group. If the children
complete their homework on time, they will receive a sticker for their
homework booklet and they will receive a second sticker to be placed on

the homework completion board (described below). Each child will have a homework book in which to keep their homework forms and to place their stickers. Next, the therapist explains the rules of the group as follows: "Even though we'll be playing games and working together, this is still a class and we need to follow regular classroom rules. In order that we can cooperate and get things done, the most important rule is that only one person talks at a time. What are some other rules that we will need to follow?" The children then generate other rules for the group. Next, the therapist describes the format of the group and the procedures to be used (i.e., instructions, modeling, feedback, rehearsal, reinforcement) and then introduces the four step Thinking Aloud Program by showing cards with the following steps:

#1 What is the problem?
#2 What can I do about it?
#3 Is it working?
#4 How did I do?

The therapist then models use of the four steps in simple situations (e.g., what comes next game, math problem). Each child is given a card with the four steps on it. The therapist then asks the children to pick a name for the group. Following this, the therapist explains the project for the day: a) to put the group name and names of group members on the homework chart, and b) to write the group rules on construction paper and post them.

Manipulation Check: Children will repeat four steps of thinking aloud and state the purpose of the group.

Homework: Homework cards are presented as follows: "Next week we'll be talking about something you do all the time. We'll be talking about carrying on a conversation. For homework, I want you to write down a time when you had an interesting conversation and tell: a) who you had the conversation with, and b) what you talked about.

Homework Card # 1

My name is: _____
I had a conversation with: _____
and, we talked about: _____

Session 2

Objectives:
1) Review treatment strategies (e.g., modeling, thinking aloud)
2) Introduce nonverbal components of conversation
3) Introduce four stages of conversation
4) Introduce concepts of sharing, cooperation and turn-taking in context of skills training.

Activities:
1) Homework review
2) Word game
3) Role play "getting to know you" game
4) Homework # 2

Materials:
1) Homework cards
2) Word game cards
3) "Getting-to-know-you" game cards
4) Stickers

Procedure: Session 2 begins with review of Homework #1, selection of stickers and posting of successful completion of homework on the homework board. Next, the therapist reviews the four steps of thinking aloud. In this and in all subsequent sessions, the concepts of cooperation, sharing, and turn-taking will be attended to as the therapist instructs and models these behaviors. Children will also be required to practice these skills throughout the course of training. The therapist instructs the children in use of nonverbal components of conversation (e.g., eye contact, response latency, tone of voice, facial expression, speech fluency). The therapist then models thinking aloud: "Step #1 — I want to figure out how the person I am talking to is feeling. Step #2 — Well, I'll check and see if they are looking at me, how long it takes them to answer my questions, how loud they are talking, whether they look and sound sad, happy, or bored, and whether they talk using a lots of 'ums' and 'uh.' (Now the therapist picks a child to talk with and describes the above mentioned nonverbal components.) (Now the therapist picks a child to talk with and describes the above-mentioned nonverbal components.) Step #3 — I seem to be figuring out how they feel and whether they are interested in talking with me. Step #4 — I did a good job. I used my four steps and paid close attention to the person I was talking to. Next, the therapist should demonstrate a "poor job" (e.g., forgetting a step, not attending to all the components) and have the group members give feedback and evaluate his or her performance.
Therapist: Now, we're going to play a game called the "Word Game." I'm going to give each of you a slip of paper with a word on it and your job is

to take turns with your partner (assign pairs) talking for 1½ minutes on whatever is on your paper. The person listening should pay attention not to *what* your partner says, but *how* she or he says it. On your sheets are listed different ways of talking that can help you get along with other people — looking at the person, tone of voice, how loud you talk, your facial expression and whether you can talk without too many "uh's . . . um's . . . ". Okay, ready? (Distribute sheets, assign one of partners to start). #1, go ahead! (After 1½ minutes, stop and discuss performance. Same procedure for #2.) Instruct children giving feedback to begin by what they *liked* about the performance and have them tell the performer directly (i.e., "*You* did a good job looking at me"). Now, the therapist instructs the children on the four stages of a conversation (greeting, small talk, main topic, closing). The therapist should model at least two conversations: one using all four stages, and one forgetting at least one stage. Children should be encouraged to give feedback and evaluate the therapist's performance. Additionally, the therapist should use the thinking aloud steps during this (e.g., "Step #1 — I want to have a conversation with Bill. Step #2 — Well, I'll go up, look right at him, talk aloud enough, and try not to say 'um' *and* I'll go through all four stages of the conversation. Step #3 — He seems to be interested in talking with me because he's looking at me and smiling. Step #4 — I did a good job. I remembered to think aloud and to use all four stages of a conversation and to pay attention to Bill.) Children should now practice conversations. As two children role-play, have the other group members signal the beginning of each phase. Be sure they can identify the main topic. Be sure to elicit feedback from other members. Finally, have each group members involved in conversation summarize their partners conversational content (i.e., listening skills). To ensure variety of main topic content, you should have one of the role-playing dyads choose a "getting-to-know-you" card. Each card will list a subject which is to serve as the main topic for the role-played conversation. Also, assign children to watch for nonverbal components discussed at the beginning of each session.

Manipulation Check:

The therapist should briefly review what has been covered in each session. The therapist should model two or three short conversations and have the children evaluate their performance on the basis of nonverbal skills, use of thinking aloud, and use of the four stages of conversation.

Homework:

Homework Assignment #2 "You are to be a detective. What you're looking for are clues that tell you how a person is feeling. During the next week, record a time when you were able to identify how someone was feeling by the way he or she looked or talked. Record this on the cards.''

Homework Card # 2

I think the person was feeling _____

_____

_____

I could tell they were feeling _____

because ( ) they were smiling
         ( ) they were frowning
         ( ) they were yawning
         ( ) they looked at me
         ( ) they didn't look at me
         ( ) they used many 'ums' and 'uhs'
         ( ) they sounded happy
         ( ) they sounded sad
         ( ) they sounded nervous

Session 3

Objectives:	1) Continue conversation skills
	2) Introduce affect recognition
	3) Integrate affect recognition with conversation skills
	4) Continue turntaking, sharing and cooperation
Activities:	1) Homework review
	2) Identifying affect from pictures
	3) Pantomiming affects
	4) Structured role plays
	5) Homework #3
Materials:	1) Homework cards
	2) Affect recognition pictures
	3) Affect recognition cards
	4) Role play situation cards
	5) Stickers

Procedure: Session 3 begins with review of Homework #2, selection of stickers, and posting of successful completion. Next, the therapist reviews the four stages of conversation and the nonverbal components associated with having a conversation. The therapist should then have the children practice brief conversations with each other. The therapist introduces concept of affect recognition and explains its importance. Then he or she shows a picture of a happy person and a sad person. Step #1 — I want to ask one of these people to help me with my homework. Step #2 — I'll try and figure out how each feels. This one is looking, down, has slumped shoulders and is frowning. The other one has a big smile on his face and his eyes are open wide. I'd ask the second one to help me because he looks happy, not sad, or grumpy. Step #3 — yes, I'm figuring out who to ask. Step #4 — I did well looking at the picture and figuring out how the person felt. The therapist shows a series of pictures of people displaying different affects and has children use the process mentioned above to identify each.

Therapist: To see how good you are at acting, we can play a game. I have cards here — which have different feelings on them. Each one of you will take one and act it out for the group. (Have each child act out an affect — give feedback and quiz others in "how did you know he was feeling that way"? If time permits, reshuffle the cards and redistribute.)

Therapist: It's important to be a detective and to look for all clues. They tell you what's going on with a person. Next, the therapist introduces structured role play situations in which the actors assume different affects and engage in conversations. The therapist models one or two situations (e.g., having a conversation with the teacher about getting the highest grade on your math: affect = happy, excited). Children should evaluate the use of the four stages of conversational thinking aloud, nonverbals, and attempt to identify affect. The therapist should model an inappropriate affect (e.g. affect = anger in situation when best friend buys you an ice cream cone). Following this, children should role play the remaining situations and give feedback regarding performances.

Manipulation Check:
The therapist should briefly review information presented. Then he or she should have the children pantomime and identify a number of different types of emotions.

Homework:
The child is asked to look through a magazine or newspaper and cut out a picture for each word. Beside each, he or she should write down how you know the person is feeling that way.

Homework Card #3

I know they feel happy because   I know they feel sad because

_____   _____

_____   _____

_____   _____

I know they feel   I know they feel

_____   _____

_____   _____

_____   _____

Session 4

Objectives: 1) Continue affect recognition
                    2) Introduce group entry skills
                    3) Continue sharing, turntaking and cooperation
Activities: 1) Homework review
                    2) Group entry task
                    3) Discussion of prosocial skills
                    4) Group anagrams
                    5) Homework #4
Materials: 1) Homework cards
                    2) Anagrams
                    3) Stickers

Procedures: Session 4 begins with homework review, selection of stickers, and posting of successful completion. The therapist should briefly review affect recognition and its importance. Next, the therapist introduces group entry task and instructs the children regarding appropriate and inappropriate ways of entering groups. The therapist should model both appropriate and inappropriate attempts to enter a group, making sure to first go through thinking aloud. The children should be encouraged to evaluate/give feedback regarding the therapist's performance. Next, the therapist should assign one child to be the "entry child" and have that child leave the group. The remainder of the children and the therapist will each assume a different emotion, and it will be the entry child's task to attempt to enter the group using thinking aloud and identifying the different affects in order to pick the "best" person to approach. This approach should continue so that each child has a chance to role play with an entry child. Then the therapist should introduce the group anagram task and discuss model cooperation, turn-taking, and sharing in this context. The therapist should first model these behaviors and then allow the children to practice. The first child to solve an anagram is to share his or her strategy with the other children.

Group Anagrams:

sharing	R A H G N S I
cooperation	N A P O C O E I T O R
friend	E N R D I F
conversation	A R V O N C O I E N T S
taking turns	K A G N I T S R N U T
problem	L R P E M O B

Manipulation Check:
   The therapist should briefly review the information presented. Then he or she should read situations that follow and have the children evaluate how the people in the situation might feel, and how they would go about entering the group, (e.g. you come into social studies class and the teacher has divided the class into groups. One group is missing recess, and the other group is missing a really hard math class to stay and finish up their social studies. How would you figure out which group to join? How would each group feel? What would you do to enter the group?)

Homework Card # 4
Write down a time when you tried to join a group of kids. What happened? _____

How did you decide what to do? _____

Session 5

Objectives:	1) Introduce role-taking
	2) Continue turn-taking, cooperation and sharing
	3) Review previously acquired skills
Activities:	1) Block game
	2) Acting out and switching roles
	3) Homework #5
Materials:	1) Homework cards
	2) Blocks
	3) Screen
	4) Character name tags
	5) Stickers

Procedure: Session 5 begins with a review of Homework #4, selection of stickers, and posting of successful completion. The therapist briefly reviews the group entry. Then he or she introduces the concept of role-taking or perspective-taking — seeing things through someone else's eyes or "walking a mile in someone else's shoes." To begin, the therapist instructs the children in the "block game." In this game one person builds a structure to another person in order that he or she could replicate it. First, the therapist should model both the correct and incorrect ways of playing the block game using thinking aloud. Children should be encouraged to give feedback and evaluate the therapist's performance. Finally children should each practice the skill by playing the game.

Introducing the play: The therapist should make the purpose of the play clear from the beginning. Thus, two points should be covered prior to the commencement of the play: 1) the idea of pretending to be someone else, and 2) viewing the situation from another person's eyes. An example of an adequate introductory statement might proceed as follows: *Therapist:* Now we are going to do something that I think you all will enjoy. Does anyone know who Lou Ferrigno is? (Child response.) That's right, he's the Incredible Hulk. Do you know what he is in real life? (Child response.) Yes, he's a weight lifter, so when you see him on T.V. as the Incredible Hulk, he's really just pretending, like all actors and actresses. (Allow children to bring up other examples.) Well, today we're going to do something very much like Lou Ferrigno does when he becomes the Hulk. We're going to act out a play and each of you will be an actor or actress. Next the therapist introduces a short play in which the children take on different roles and at specified points in the play each actor or actress will be asked to assume a new role and explain the situation from the new role's perspective. Now we are going to do a short play. In this one we will be following the same rules, that is, having Stops and Switches, but the scene will be a little different this time. Now, let's pretend we are right here at _____ Elementary School. Here's the situation:

Characters:
Teacher
Student #1
Student #2
Student #3
Principal
Audience

Scene: You (Student #1) are the first one back to the classroom following recess and as you go into the classroom, you see someone you don't know (Student #2) at the teacher's desk. When student #2 sees you he/ she rushes out of the room and knocks books and papers off the teacher's desk. You are wondering what he or she was doing there and go over to pick up the things off the floor. Student #3 comes in and asks what you're doing. While you try to explain, the teacher enters the room and asks what you're doing with his or her things. She gets angry and accuses you of being at the desk without his or her permission. She asks the other student what happened. When the teacher realizes that he or she is missing a book she calls the principal. (Discuss stages, affect in general fashion, take turns role-playing various characters).

Manipulation Check:
The therapist briefly reviews role-taking. The therapist shows children, one at a time, a common object (e.g., pencil, chalk, table) and has one child describe it to another child (who can't see the object).

Homework:
Have the children pick a comic book or T.V. hero and write down what he or she would do or say.

Homework Card # 5
Pick a comic book or T.V. hero and write down the things that he or she does so we can figure out who you are _____
_____
_____

Session 6
Objectives: 1) Continue role-taking
                         2) Continue sharing, cooperation, and turn-taking
                         3) Review of previously required skills
Activities: 1) Homework cards
                         2) Structured play
                         3) Homework #6
Materials: 1) Homework cards
                         2) Props
                         3) Stickers

Procedure: Session 6 begins with review of Homework #5, selection of stickers, and posting of successful completion. Therapist briefly reviews role-taking and models one or two situations, requiring children to give feedback and evaluate therapist's performance. Therapist then allows children to practice by introducing a new play. Our play will be about a land of kings and princesses. All of you will get a part to play. In our play, it is very important to really become the character, just like Lou does when he's the Incredible Hulk. You have to forget that you are Susie or Johnny and *become* the king or the princess. This is important because we will be stopping from time to time and asking how you feel and what you see happening. When we do that, we want to know how the princess feels and what she sees, not what you, Susie or Kathy, might be feeling. So when I say "Stop" what will you do? (Child response.) Good, I think you've got the idea. In addition, we will also be doing one other thing. From time to time I will hold up this flag (any item can be used as a signal). When I do that I want each of you to switch parts with someone else. I will tell you which role you will take. It is very important that you listen carefully and really pretend to be the person.

Characters:
King
Princess
Valoose (person from outer space -- planet Ziron)
Court Jester
Judge
Jury Members (any number of children who are left)
Props:
toy goose
flag (or other signal)
scripts (enough for half of the group members)

The therapist is free to use his or her imagination in selecting and bringing in props to be used in the play. For example, crowns or tiaras can easily be made from cardboard and aluminum foil. Antennas can be used for "Valoose." A gavel or robe might be given to the judge, and the jester may wear a pointed hat. The jurors might be provided with signs to put around their necks. The use of props adds color and excitement to the play and facilitates in gaining the children's interest and involvement. However, it is equally important to ensure that the main focus of the play is to disseminate information on the concept of role-taking. Therefore, elaborate props should be avoided as they may distract from the essence of the activity. We generally recommend one prop per character.

Therapist: "Remember, after the switch, I'll be asking you how you feel and what you see going on, only this time you'll have to become the 'new' person, and explain it from the new person's point of view. So, for example, Mike, if you were the king and then switched to a jury member, what would you have to do? (Child response.) That's right, you would quickly change costumes and explain what's going on from the jury member's point of view, forgetting what you knew and felt as king. Are there any questions? Then we're ready to begin." (Following introduction, the children are all assigned roles and the play proceeds as follows). *Scene:* The play takes place in the land of kings, princesses, and magical geese. The goose is extremely valuable because it lays golden eggs. The goose belongs to the king and he treasures it and will not let anyone come near it. The king's daughter, the princess, has always been very fond of the goose and for years has begged the king to let her keep the goose in her room. He has always refused. Finally, this very day in *December*, the king agreed to let her keep the goose but she will be held responsible. The princess is delighted and cheerfully takes the goose to her room. On her way to her room she sees the Court Jester in the hallway. He is doing tricks. She has always thought him very mischievous.

> *Jester:* Hello, Princess, and how are you today?
> *Princess:* Fine, thank you. See what I have? I'm to keep the Golden Goose.
> *Jester:* Oh, you are, are you? And how grand of the king to let you care for his most valued possession.
> The princess goes into her room and watches the Golden Goose very carefully, for she wants to be sure that nothing bad happens to him. Finally, after a few minutes, she becomes thirsty and hungry.
> *Princess:* I think I'll go out to get a bite to eat. But I shall not take the Golden Goose for fear he'll fly away while I fix a sandwich. I dare not leave him alone in my room either; he might fly out the window. What can I do? I know, I'll place him in the storage room in the

hall for only a few minutes until I get back. He shall be safe there.

She places the Goose in the storage room and goes to make a sandwich. Meanwhile, Valoose has landed in his spaceship a mere stone's throw from the castle in which the king and princess live. He, too, has a goose, but on the planet Ziron (from which Valoose comes), they are called "zeese" (or, "zoose" for one). Valoose goes out exploring this new planet and, lo and behold, his zoose (named Roose) flies away. Valoose is very upset and goes to find him. He comes upon the king's castle and says:

> *Valoose:* I bet my zoose, Roose, went in there to get something to eat. I shall have to go and find him.

Actually, Roose the zoose has flown back to the spaceship and is awaiting Valoose there. Valoose goes into the castle and finally into the hallway where the Golden Goose is hidden in the storage room. There is no sign of Roose and Valoose begins to get discouraged. Just as he is about to leave, he hears a noise.

> *Valoose:* What's that noise? Why, it sounds like my zoose, Roose. I believe it's coming from behind that door!

So Valoose checks to see that no one is around and then slowly opens the door.

> *Valoose:* Aha! There you are, Roose, my beloved zoose! Actually, it was the goose and not zoose named Roose. Valoose takes the goose (which he thinks is Roose) and quickly flees from the castle. About this time, the princess has finished her sandwich and says:

> *Princess:* I'm quite full now, I think I'll go back to my room. Oh! I'll take a dish of mousse for the Golden Goose.

As she enters the hallway, she catches a glimpse of the Court Jester leaving at the opposite end.

> *Princess:* Oh no! I hope the goose is still there! She rushes down the hallway, and, alas, the Golden Goose is gone.

> *Princess:* Whatever shall I do? My father, the king, entrusted me with his most prized possession and it is gone. I bet the Jester has him! But it is too late tonight and there is nothing I can do. I'll have to wait until morning.

STOP! !

Therapist asks questions about the situations and feelings of the various characters. Be sure that the characters report the situation and feelings appropriate to their information. Also, elicit information and feelings from judge and jury members. What are the characters thoughts here — what might they be saying to themselves? How could they change how they feel? What new thoughts could they have?

SWITCH! !

Scene: Next day: The princess goes to the king and explains the situation. Prior to having the princess explain the situation, the therapist should have the child verbalize the first two of the four self-statements. That is, 1) What is the problem? ("I need to explain to my father what has happened to the Golden Goose"), and 2) What am I going to do? ("I'm going to tell him that something serious has happened and then explain

what I know step by step.") As the child proceeds, he or she should be reinforced for adherence to his or her plan and prompted when (s)he deviates. Also, in the course of carrying out his/her plan, the two remaining cognitive steps should be addressed; 3) Is my plan working? (Have the child attend to the reaction of the king and see how well the plan is working. If it is working, reinforce; if not, return to step 2 and generate another plan), and 4) How did I do? Have the child orally report on his or her performance and evaluate his or her use of the cognitive strategy noting changes that had to be made on the initial plan, and reinforce him or herself. Note that the emphasis is on: 1) thinking about what action to take and evaluating its likely consequences before implementing its *actual* consequences and changing or proceeding accordingly.
STOP!

Therapist asks questions following the procedure above.

Later that same day:
The king decides to hold court to find out what happened to the Golden Goose. Enter Judge and Jury.
(After 3 to 4 minutes of ad-libbing, SWITCH) From here, the play continues according to the children's fantasy. The therapist should use his/her judgment in deciding what issues merit clarification or elaboration, and should intervene accordingly. He or she may use several more Stops and Switches if desired and deemed to be productive.
STOP!

The therapist asks questions about the situation and the feelings of the various characters. What thoughts might influence these feelings? Be sure that the characters report situation and feelings that correspond with the information that the particular character has. Also, elicit information and feelings from judge and jury members. What is the judge saying to him or herself?

Manipulation Check:
   The therapist briefly reviews role-taking. The therapist reads a short story and then questions children about how the people might be feeling. "Susan has been working really hard on her art project for the school fair. She even stayed after school yesterday to put on the finishing touches. When Susan gets to school the next day she sees her art project lying, broken, on the floor. Two kids from her class are standing nearby looking at the broken artwork. Susan accuses the two kids of ruining her project. Just then the principal walks around the corner towards Susan."

Homework:
Have children write about a time when their parents disciplined them.

Homework Card #6

1) *How do your parents feel when they discipline you?*

_____

2) *How do you feel when your parents discipline you?*

3) *How do your brothers and/or sisters feel when your parents discipline you?*

Session 7

Objectives:	1) Continue role-taking
	2) Introduce negative assertion
	3) Continue sharing, cooperation, turn-taking
Activities:	1) Review
	2) Role playing
	3) Homework #7
Materials:	1) Homework cards
	2) Situation cards
	3) Stickers

Procedure: Session 7 begins with review of Homework #6, selection of stickers and posting of successful completion. The therapist briefly reviews role-taking. Then he or she introduces concept of negative assertion in context of standing up for one's own rights. The therapist models appropriate and inappropriate ways of standing up for one's rights, and encourages children to give feedback and evaluate their performance. For example:

Therapist: You just started playing with a new toy. A boy comes over to you and says "give me that toy right now! I want to play with it."
ECSS—F

Step 1   "What's the problem . . . that boy wants me to give him my toy but I'm not finished playing with it."

Step 2   "What can I do about it? . . . I'll look him in the eye and say in a firm voice I just started playing with it. You can have it as soon as I'm finished."

Step 3   "Is it working? . . . Yes, I'm still playing with the toy. I told the boy 'no' without getting angry and upset and offered to let him use the toy when I'm done."

Step 4   "How did I do? . . . I did a pretty good job. I used 'thinking aloud' and told the boy 'no'."

The therapist should have children take turns role playing other situations (provided by the therapist and/or suggested by children) and evaluating each other's performance. It is important to allow the children to practice skills until they perform appropriately. Specific feedback and modeling should be provided by the therapist.

Manipulation Check:

The therapist briefly reviews negative assertion. Each child is to role play a short situation requiring negative assertion.

Homework:

Have the children write down a time when they got blamed for something they didn't do.

Homework Card # 7

Name _____

I got blamed for something I didn't do. It was _____

_____ . What I did _____

_____ . When it happened I was saying to myself ___

myself _____

OR

A friend asked me to do something I didn't want to do. It was

_____ . What I did _____ .

When it happened I was saying to myself _____

Session 8

Objectives:	1) Continue negative assertion
	2) Continue sharing, cooperation, and turn-taking
Activities:	1) Review homework
	2) Role play game
	3) Homework #8
Materials:	1) Homework cards
	2) Situation cards
	3) Stickers

Procedures: Session begins with homework review, selection of stickers, and posting of successful completion. The therapist begins by reviewing negative assertion and modeling appropriate and inappropriate responses. Children should be encouraged to give feedback and evaluate his or her performance. To introduce a variant into the usual role play procedure, this session should be presented as a game. Like Session 7, two children will be involved in a role play scenario, requiring negative assertion skills. Children will take turns choosing the scenarios which will be written on pieces of construction paper and concealed within a box. Unlike Session 7, however, each of the other children will be assigned one area to watch for the score according to how well he or she thinks the "actor" fulfilled the requirement. The scorers will rate the target child on a scale of 1 to 5 (1 — needs much improvement; 5 — very good job) on each of the following areas: 1) initial plan formulation (plan), 2) use of the plan, 3) self-evaluation plan, 4) verbal content, 5) nonverbal behavior. These categories (with rewarding) can be written on a blackboard with the scorer's name. One child can be appointed to write up scores for each scene. Duties are switched until every child has had a chance to be the "actor/actress." Briefly, initial plan formulations should assess the quality of the child's verbal plan prior to initiation of the interaction. Use of the plan should refer to how well the child actually followed through on what he or she said he or she was going to do. Self-evaluation of the plan is an assessment of the child's ability to adapt and revise his or her plan in the face of unforeseen opposition or negative reaction. Verbal content refers to the verbal performance aspect (what was said). Nonverbal behavior should include overt nonverbal indices of performance expression; or, *how* he or she said it. The advantages of the game format are many. First, it provides some variety from the usual role play procedures, and thus engages the children's interest. Secondly, the introduction of a score may motivate the children to do well and thus give the therapist the opportunity to observe and assess their abilities to perform the trained skills. Third, the children are receiving quantifiable feedback which gives them a basis of comparison when looking from one skill to another (e.g., eye contact, verbal content). It will indicate to them the areas they need to work on the hardest.

Finally, the game format provides an excellent opportunity for the therapist to observe the performance of other skills trained earlier in the program such as sharing, turn-taking, and cooperation in a relatively natural and uncontrived situation.

Manipulation check:

The therapist briefly reviews negative assertion. Each child is to role play short situation requiring negative assertion.

Homework:

Next the children should write down a time in the next week when someone treated them unfairly.

Homework Card # 8

For next week. I want you to write down a time when someone treats you unfairly and you have to say "no" to them . Some examples are someone taking something of yours without your permission, someone taking your turn to kick at kickball, or someone asking you to do something that you feel to be unreasonable. Since it has to be a situation that happens in the next week, you'll have to keep an eye open for such a time and remember to do what we've been talking about in here when it happens. After writing down the situation, score how well you did on a scale of 1 to 5 on each of the areas listed on your Homework Card:

1) plan
2) how well you used the plan
3) how well the plan worked
4) verbal content (what you said)
5) nonverbal aspects (looking at the person, talking in a firm voice, staying calm, not using too many 'ums' and ('uhs')

Session 9

Objectives:	1) Introduce positive assertion
	2) Continue sharing, cooperation, and turn-taking
Activities:	1) Review homework
	2) Role playing
	3) Homework #9

Materials   1) Homework cards
                          2) Situation cards
                          3) Stickers

Procedure: Session begins with homework review, selection of stickers, and posting of successful completion. The therapist introduces concept of positive assertion in the context of giving and receiving compliments, and in asking to join activities. The therapist models appropriate and inappropriate ways of giving and receiving compliments and joining activities and encourages children to give feedback and evaluate his or her performance. For example: *Therapist*: A group of kids are playing a game of kickball on the playground. You'd like to play too. Then, the therapist models the self instruction procedure. *Step 1* What's the problem? . . . Some kids are playing kickball and I'd like to play too. *Step 2* What can I do about it? . . . I'll go up to the kids and watch for a minute then go over to a kid who looks friendly, look him in the eye, smile and ask if I could (plays this response with a child) *Step 3* Is it working? . . . Yes, I figure out which kid looked nice and friendly and he seems to want me to play. *Step 4* How did I do? I did a good job. I used thinking aloud and I smiled and looked the kid in the eye when I asked.

    The therapist then brings out a bag with the situation cards inside. Each child picks a card and goes through the self instruction procedure and then acts out the appropriate alternative two times. Specific feedback and modeling should be provided by the therapist.

Manipulation Check:
    Therapist briefly reviews positive assertion. Each child should role play a short situation requiring positive assertion.

Homework:
    Finally, the therapist passes out homework cards with the following instruction. "I want you to ask a classmate for help in school. I also want you to tell me whether it was hard or easy to do that, and how you used thinking aloud."

Homework Card # 9

Name _____

I asked _____ *to help me do* _____

_____ *in* _____ *class. I used*

thinking aloud by _____ .

Session 10
Objectives: 1) Continue positive assertion
                         2) Continue sharing, cooperation, and turn-taking
Activities: 1) Review homework
                         2) Role play game
                         3) Homework |# 10
Materials: 1) Homework cards
                         2) Situation cards
                         3) Stickers

Procedures: Session begins with homework review, selection of stickers, and posting of successful completion. The therapist reviews positive assertion and models both appropriate and inappropriate responses. Children should be encouraged to give feedback and evaluate the therapist's performance. To introduce a variant into the role play procedure, this session should be presented as a game. As in Session #9, two children will act out role play scenarios requiring positive assertion skills. Children will take turns choosing the scenarios which will be written on pieces of construction paper and concealed within a box. Unlike before, however, each of the remaining group members will be assigned one area to watch for and score according to how well (s)he thinks the "actor" performed. The scorers will rate the target child on a scale 1-5 (1 — needs much improvement; 5 — very good job) on each of the following areas:

1) plan
2) how well was the plan used
3) how well did the plan work
4) verbal content
5) nonverbal behaviors (eye contact, voice introduction, and body posture)

These categories (with rewording) can be written on a blackboard alone with children's names. One child can be appointed to write up scores for each scene. Duties are switched until every child has had an opportunity to be the "actor/actress." The advantages of the game format were detailed in Session 8.

Manipulation Check:
   The therapist briefly reviews positive assertion. Each child should role play a short situation requiring positive assertion.

Homework:
The child should be asked to write a time in the next week when they complimented someone.

Homework Card # 10

For next week, I want you to write down a time that happens between now and next week that you went up and complimented someone for something he or she did well. Then I want you to give yourself a score on a scale of 1 to 5 on each of the areas listed on the back of the Homework Card:

1) plan
2) how well you used your plan
3) how well the plan worked
4) verbal content (what you said)
5) non-verbal aspects (looking at the person, smiling, not using too many 'ums' and 'uhs,' sounding happy).

Session 11

Objectives:	1) Integrate skills
Activities:	1) Review homework
	2) Blind traveler game
	3) Nerf basketball
	4) Structured role plays
	5) Homework # 11
Materials:	1) Homework cards
	2) Nerf basketball
	3) Blindfold
	4) Crepe paper
	5) Stickers

Procedures: Session begins with homework review, selection of stickers, and posting of successful completion. The therapist will instruct children in the blind traveler game and nerf basketball. Description of blind travelers game: Objects are placed around the room on the floor and at table level. Children take turns being the 'blind traveler.' The group members spread out to different areas of the room. A child is chosen by the therapist, blindfolded, and turned "around and around" so that the child is not sure of his or her orientation. Crepe paper strips are placed on the floor and on a few tables. These are "poisonous snakes." If the blind traveler touches them, then the guides have failed in the their task.

The therapist writes on the board the name of the object to which the traveler must be guided. The guides take turns giving one sentence descriptions of what the traveler must do to reach the object and, most importantly, to avoid obstacles along the way. The children are encouraged to give supportive statements (compliments) to both the guiders and traveler. Nerf basketball game: Team *Horse*.

Therapist: Now we are going to divide up into two teams and play a game which involves shooting this nerf basketball into this waste paper basket. Each time a team misses a shot, the team gets a letter. When a team gets all five letters (h o r s e), they lose. One person on each team will stand behind this line and another person on each team will stand behind this line on the other side of the room, and hold the basket. When your teammate shoots, you can move the can to catch the ball. And here is the most important part, each of you must say at least two good things about how your teammates do. That is, during the game I have to hear you tell your teammates that they did something good or right; I have to hear you at least twice. I'll be keeping score of that here. Any questions? Let's go ahead. During these games therapist should set up different situations in which the children can use the skills presented thus far. For example, the therapist might cut in line in front of one of the children. Children should be instructed to set up role play situations with each other. Additionally, aspects of ongoing activity should be used to structure role plays (e.g., cooperation during the blind traveler game).

Homework:
Have children write down what they did and didn't like about the group.

Homework Card # 11

What I liked: 1) _____

                           2) _____

                           3) _____

What I didn't like: 1) _____

                           2) _____

                           3) _____

Because of this group I have found it easier to make friends
(1) not at all
(2) a little
(3) some
(4) quite a bit
(5) a lot

Session 12

Objectives: 1) Assessment of social skills
                    2) Continued rehearsal of skills
                    3) Provide closure
Activities: 1) Social skills game
                    2) Review of homework #11
Materials: 1) Social skills Game
                    2) Stickers

Procedures: The group leader explains the objectives of the making friends games (the social skills game was designed for the project). The objective of the game is for each player to advance around the board in a clockwise direction by amassing points earned through appropriate responses to problems, questions, or role play scenarios, posed by the game. Each player begins at block #1 and receives five stickers to start. Each player rolls the dice with the highest role determining who takes the first turn. As a player lands on a space, he or she follows the instructions or draws a card from the designated pile in the center of the board. Stack A contains cards designed to assess the players *knowledge* of information pertaining to conversation, role-taking, and positive and negative assertiveness. These cards will pose fill-in, multiple-choice, yes-no, true-false questions to the player. Stack B contains cards designed to assess a player's specific *cognitive* (i.e., the four stages of think aloud and *behavioral* responses germane to these same skills). These cards will pose role play scenarios in which players will engage in interactions with another player, as instructed. For example, in the case of affect recognition, the player will be asked to identify the person's affect (How does this person feel?") and also to explain how he or she came to that conclusion ("What is it about this person that makes you think that he or she is _____?"). Thus, the objective is for the player to reach some reasonable conclusion regarding the affect of the person in the picture *and* to explain how he or she reached that conclusion (e.g., eyes open wide, smile, etc.), rather than to surmise an objectively correct affect. Stack C contains cards designed to add variety to the game by providing for the *possible* loss of accumulated stickers. These cards list descriptions of situations in which the player is said to have been involved. The player is said to have responded unassertively/inappropriately to a positive or negative assertion situation and is designated a loss of stickers. The player may prevent the loss of stickers by describing an assertive/appropriate response to the situation. Each player's responses to a question or scenario are judged to be appropriate by other members of the group (e.g., "Is Jim right?" Why or Why not?), although the group leader will serve as the ultimate judge. If a player successfully completes the assigned task, then he or she receives the allotted stickers. If he or she does not complete the task successfully, the player does not receive the stickers and the appropriate responses is discussed by the group. As the game proceeds, players accumulate stickers respectively. Session 12 should end with discussion of Homework #11 to provide closure for the groups. Children will be given their completed homework booklets and the stickers they earned for successful homework completion. Finally, the children will be encouraged to continue to use the skill acquired and to share those skills with their friends.

SUMMARY

In this chapter, we have reviewed a variety of issues associated with the development and implementation of a social skill curiculum for children. Among the issues addressed were factors related to the characteristics of the children identified for treatment and the precise nature of their social skill deficit, the content and processes of the training procedures, and how best to evaluate the success of the program. Although a cognitive social learning approach was highlighted, we concluded that that there are various approaches available and that there is no "one" way to conduct social skills training.

Chapter 5
Special Populations and Considerations

INTRODUCTION

Most books on child psychology and education deal almost exclusively with children who do not have physical or intellectual handicaps. This omission is unfortunate, since handicapped children make up an important and sizable segment of children who are seen by professionals for social adjustment problems. In addition, given recent litigation, the courts have mandated that closer and greater attention be given to these persons. It should be pointed out from the outset that various handicapped groups have special needs to be addressed. Dependent upon the special handicap, adaptations will be necessary.

Having said this, much of what has been done with the general population of children with regard to social skills assessment and treatment should prove useful in the adaptation of procedures to the groups discussed below. Here, we address specific intervention for mentally retarded, visually impaired, and hearing impaired children.

MENTALLY RETARDED

Social skills deficits are a defining characteristic of mental retardation (Grossman, 1983). This fact would seem evident when one considers the lack of intellectual ability and general social retardation particularly in the mildly mentally retarded group. There is considerable recognition that mentally retarded persons require assistance in social behavior, and researchers have documented this hypothesis in a great deal of recent

83

research (Andrasik & Matson, 1985). One opinion about this problem is that persons with mental retardation are at risk because of cognitive limitations which lead to a lack of understanding about how to behave in various social settings (Greenspan, 1979). No doubt this is a major concern, and certainly it is a strong argument for developing social skills assessment and training strategies for this group.

In the field of mental retardation, the range of behaviors defined as social in content is far beyond that of any other group. For example, the American Association on Mental Deficiency Adaptive Behavior Scale has described toileting and hygiene as social skills (Nihira et al. 1974). This trend is not in line with the general field and the extensive body of research developed in the area of social skills, but it is changing toward a focus on interpersonal behavior as research and training begins to escalate with this group.

It should be pointed out that the specific behaviors treated are likely to vary more with this population than any other group treated. Mildly mentally retarded persons, for example, may vary somewhat, but generally the problems of these children are similar to what is seen with most children. These responses include eye contact, appropriate content of speech, sharing, helping others, voice volume, talking loudly, and pestering others. With many profoundly mentally retarded persons, the target responses do not include words and may be the group where the most adaptations of available procedures are needed to ensure meaningful assessment and treatment. However, nonverbal responses that denote yes, no, and so on might be shaped and reinforced, as well as eye contact, head orientation, and appropriate facial affect. These interactions can be very important and can dramatically increase the social interactions of these persons given that their ability to make contact with the environment may be limited.

It should be noted that operant conditioning and social learning are the two major training methods used with persons who are mentally retarded. As a general rule of thumb, approaches that incorporate social learning theory are used more often with persons who have greater intellectual abilities, the more severely intellectually impaired are more likely to be treated with operant conditioning methods, usually in small and discrete behavioral units. Typical of the operant methods is an early study conducted by Whitman et al. (1970). They worked with two severely mentally retarded, withdrawn children. Training occured in 30 sessions, wherein food and praise were delivered contingent upon the children's mutual participation in play. Other children were brought into the training situations at certain points in an attempt to facilitate generalization. Training produced marked increases in social responding that generalized to children not involved in training. These findings are very encouraging, since it has been only recently that these children have been viewed as being likely to improve in social skills. Other investigators have found similarly positive effects through the use of primary, token, and or social reinforcers for improving interpersonal behavior (Barton, 1973; Deutsch & Parks, 1978; Luiselli et al. 1978).

Two examples of the social learning methods described in Chapters 3 and 4 will also be mentioned. These methods are the most recently researched and may have a good future for remediating social inadequacies of mentally retarded children. Matson et al. (1980) conducted one study that exemplifies this trend. They treated two boys aged 11 and 12 who had been hospitalized for conduct disorder and who evinced moderate mental retardation. Various components of social skills were targeted for treatment, including gestures, mannerisms, eye contact, and intonation in speech. Treatment, which proved to be very effective, included describing situations where inappropriate behavior occured, asking for responses to these scenes, modeling correct responses, and the use of role-playing. Daily sessions of less than 30 minutes proved to be highly effective, at least in the therapy room, in dramatically improving social behavior.

Nelson et al. (1973) also demonstrated an effective social skills treatment program using social learning theory. In their case, a short-term residential care setting with a 7-year-old boy was the scene for training. Even though the child was highly expressive, significant deficits existed, such as difficulty in asking questions in a grammatically correct form, infrequent appropriate smiling and content of speech. Training procedures included modeling via videotape presentation of same age normal boys, instructions plus reinforcement and a combination of these methods. The training proved to be quite effective and suggests a variation on how best to enhance social skills.

These behavioral methods proved to be useful with mentally retarded persons evincing specification of discrete responses in a highly structured training format. However, much needs to be done before a well-defined training strategy is available for the many variations of social skills deficits and excesses displayed by these children. A suggested focus for training is teaching parents how to employ behavioral skills in the training of social behaviors with this population. Also, a strategy that has proven effective with more training strategies are needed which include teaching curriculums that can be employed with severe and profound mentally retarded childrn in the school environment. It is likely that such curriculums will rely on direct teaching as well as modeling-based procedures.

VISUALLY IMPAIRED

Some special deficit areas exist for visually handicapped children. For example, Van Hasselt et al (1985) found high rates of stereotype behaviors such as body-rocking, head-rolling, and hand-flapping, significantly longer speech delays, and high frequencies of speech disturbance with this group. Matson and associates have also found emotional problems to be more frequent in visually impaired children than in the overall population (Heinze et al., in press). However, it should also be pointed out that greater expressions of appreciation and less hostile intonation have been found with visually impaired adolescents compared to those persons without visual impairments. This point is important, since it confirms that visually handicapped persons may in fact evince superior behavior in some skill areas. For these and other problems, some important and specialized issues exist (Matson & Helsel, 1985).

Social skills training and other procedures for enhancing social skills deficits have traditionally been accomplished by communicating via visual cues. This approach, of course, is not possible when the person treated is severely visually handicapped (Farkas et al., 1981); modifications of training are needed. In the study just cited a 12½-year-old blind, psychotic girl was treated for tapping, hand-flapping, and rocking. A modification from standard behavioral program was the use of braille-coded tokens which could be exchanged for primary reinforcers via Differential Reinforcement of Other Behavior (DRO). The girl found this reinforcement scheme of considerable value and her inappropriate behavior was improved dramatically.

The traditional social skills package — modeling, direct instruction, behavioral rehearsal, performance feedback, and manual guidance — has also been employed with visually handicapped children. Van Hasselt et al. (1985) were able to improve assertiveness skills in four visually handicapped female adolescents (14 to 20 years). Each person received three to four weeks of assertiveness training in five 15 to 30-minute sessions weekly. Behaviors treated were direction of gaze, posture, voice tone, and requests for behavior change. This method and the token reinforcement approach noted above both have considerable promise for this group, since there is a large literature to draw from regarding persons with other handicaps.

A third model of intervention is a classroom intervention strategy (Sisson et al., 1984). In this case, training was given directly in the child's classroom. Of course, this can be of considerable value in promoting appropriate generalization, since training is given at the site where the skill is to be performed. Similarly, to decrease the cost and need for one-to-one training as well as to enhance modeling, peers can be involved in treatment consisting of modeling, feedback, and reinforcement. In this study four children, 9 to 11 years of age, in the same classroom were trained on increasing social initiations and positive responses. All the children treated were legally blind and/or mentally retarded or hearing impaired. A group of nonhandicapped children were training in eliciting appropriate behavior through instructions, social reinforcement and demonstration. They then assisted their visually handicapped peers in a free-play situation by modeling appropriate responses and giving feedback. Treatment of this sort has the added advantage of promoting interactions of children without handicaps and those children who are not so fortunate. While not directly measured in this study, it seems feasible that this approach may enhance the likelihood of better understanding and knowledge between children with and without sensory impairment. Currently, several research groups are working in the area of social skills training with visually handicapped persons. Therefore, it is likely that major advances will appear in this area within the near future.

HEARING IMPAIRED

The difficulties of the hearing-impaired are perceived by many as even more severe than those of the visually impaired (Matson & Helsel, 1985). In general, however, the social and emotional problems of persons with hearing impairments are much greater than for visually impaired persons and less so for persons with mental retardation.

Some information has been collected on social skills with the Matson Evaluation of Social Skills with Youngsters (MESSY). Macklin and Matson (1985) found that hearing impaired children were typically less assertive than their nonhandicapped peers. On the positive side, these children displayed appropriate affect, followed rules, and were compliant. While these data are interesting and provide some clues about social interpersonal skills with the hearing impaired, more research is clearly needed to advance this area of study.

The hearing impaired have received very little attention from researchers with respect to social skills treatment, there have been only two such efforts to date. In one of these studies Lemanek et al. (1986) treated four children and adolescents from 11 to 18 years of age. All of these children were described as socially withdrawn and were targeted for treatment on long response latency, inappropriate verbalization, and poor eye contact. All four children had a substantial hearing loss. Two of the children used sign language and two of them used oral speech as their primary means of communication. Training was conducted via a five-minute social interaction between one child and a confederate. The behaviors measured during these interactions were frequency of communication, frequency of open-ended questions, smiling, eye contact, and gestures. The training package included six major procedures: 1) the narrator described one of the 10 training scenes for that sessions and delivered a predetermined prompt to which the subject responded; 2) positive and negative feedback were given on the target behaviors; 3) instructions for appropriate responses were provided; 4) an appropriate response was modeled for the child if he or she was unable to perform the behavior; 5) behavioral rehearsal continued until sufficient performance was attained; and 6) social reinforcement was given as the subject's responses increasingly approximated the performance criterion. There were eight training sessions. Marked improvements in the discrete social responses targeted were noted and the effects were largely maintained at a two-month follow-up.

Matson et al. (1987) have taken a somewhat different approach to social skills training. Working with five autistic hearing-impaired children aged 12 to 14 years, they treated eye contact, on-task appropriate verbal content, and bizzare mannerisms. Given the severe multiple impairments — which also included mental retardation in three cases — a series of procedures were developed specifically for social skills training with these children. In cases of children with hearing impairments, a major concern is ensuring that the children are attending to visual stimuli. This goal is much more important than is the case with other groups of children, since vision is the primary mode of communication. During the 15-minute training sessions, educational materials were presented pictorially. Emphasis was placed on being able to name the pictures. However, the focus on training emphasized the target behaviors with performance feedback using sign language and pictorial representations of the skills. Also, emphasis was placed on correctly performed behaviors followed by their reinforcement. For this study a reinforcement board was used and had been developed by the senior author for a a previous study with an autistic adult. An 8 × 11 cardboard sheet with 6 to 10 items serving as common reinforcers for each child was used. The child could point to the reinforcer he or she preferred. In this way, the power of the reinforcer could be improved by allowing the child to pick the most reinforcing item for him or her at the particular point in time. Modeling and role playing of appropriate behavior, verbal and physical prompts, and social reinforcement were also used. These procedures proved to be highly effective, even with these multiply handicapped youths, further demonstrating the power of this technology.

It should be pointed out also that this study exemplifies what many professionals know to be the case: there is a substantial subset of children with multiple handicaps who may benefit from social skills training when modifications in the training technology are made.

GENERAL ISSUES

While a great deal of research is not currently available on the treatment of social skills with handicapped youth, the available research is promising. Making modifications in social skills treatment programs that have proven effective with other childhood groups have been useful with these children. Of course some modifications to the treatment plans have been necessary. Two other areas that may prove to be particularly fruitful in enhancing social skills of these children are curriculums for school ad home and parent training. When coordinated with outside psychological consultation and therapy, a powerful treatment/habilitative package is likely to result. A brief mention of these programs will follow.

CURRICULUM

Children with handicapping conditions present special problems to educators. For children with intellectual, hearing, visual or physical handicaps, many adaptations to the teaching materials and manner in which teaching is carried out must be considered. Conversely, with mentally retarded children a major focus must be the content of training (MacMillan, 1982). Having said this, little formal work has been done to date to develop specialized curriculums. And, this problem is compounded with mentally retarded persons in particular because their skill levels vary so widely. Most curriculums in this field tend to focus on three major substance areas: social competence, personal adequacy, and occupational adequacy. (Kolstoe, 1976; Kirk & Johnson, 1951). Thus, social skills cut across these populations of children and are very important for the educator to consider.

In curriculum development, three major issues should be considered for special populations: a) how likely these skills are to enhance independence and mainstreaming into the larger society; b) how the curriculum can be coordinated with parent training and efforts by other professionals, particularly psychologists outside the school; and, c) how

ECSS—G

best to implement behaviorally based curriculum.

With regard to enhancement of independent living and mainstreaming, the function of the skill should be considered and where possible the skill should be taught directly. Social validation is a useful method of determining the functional nature of the behavior (Kazdin & Matson, 1981). It is suggested that the social interpersonal skills of "normal" same-age and same-sex peers be compared and contrasted to the handicapped child. Specific skill areas such as eye contact and content of speech should be identified and where they differ markedly from the target group should be indentified for habilitation. The close handicapped children approximate the social skills of their nonhandicapped peers, the more likely they will be accepted into mainstream society. Also, appropriate assertiveness and the like should greatly enhance independence.

The second point noted was coordinating the curriculum with parents and with professionals. This can be achieved by meeting with parents and interested professionals and getting their input into curriculum plans. Helping parents design curriculums for home use can also prove to be of great value. These efforts can greatly accelerate positive change and can dramatically improve generalization and maintenance of desired skills.

The final issue is the design of a behaviorally based curriculum. Some important areas to consider in such a task are: a) delineating a behavioral objective; b) reviewing the available resources; c) deriving and sequencing the component skills of the objective; d) eliminating unnecessary and redundant component skills; e) determining what prerequisite skills are needed by the student; and, f) monitoring the student's performance and revising the skill sequence accordingly. These points provide a useful guideline. It is important to keep in mind that the curriculum involves a number of interrelated components. Social interpersonal skills should be worked where possible, into the natural sequence of academic tasks. For example, teaching speech, sign language, or other communication skills can be paired with the most socially appropriate way of using this newfound learning. Also, the teacher should start with existing skills and use these to build on already existing strengths (Payne & Patton, 1981). This combination of methods and procedures with adaptations for a child's particular handicap can prove to be most useful in establishing the training, maintenance, and generalization of social skills with these special children.

PARENT TRAINING

Perhaps the strongest proponent for parent training with the developentally disabled has been Harris (1983). She presents three arguments as to why this approach should be stressed: 1) the recognition that there are not enough professional therapists and educators to meet the needs of all who might benefit from behavioral techniques; 2) the realization that parents, as part of the natural environment, might be uniquely suited to implement some programs; and, 3) the discovery that the developmentally disabled had difficulty transferring skills learned in one setting to another context. These arguments are gaining ground. One of the best formulated and most comprehensive programs in this area, and among the first to demonstrate the value of parents as full partners in the educational process with developmentally disabled children was that developed by Schopler (1978).

Today, most of the writing and practice in this area has been with self-help skills and handling maladaptive behavior with operant conditioning techniques. However, the same structure for teaching and frame of reference could also be used if social skills are to be the major focus of the training. In one study, Koegal et al. (1977) identified five skill areas which continue to be recommended for attention when training parents: 1) clear commands; 2) well-timed reinforcers; 3) shaping of new behaviors with successive approximations; 4) effective prompts of desired responses; and, 5) utilization of discrete trials. Perhaps the more important point to make here is that a wide range of basic behavioral skills need to be trained. In our experience didactic work alone may not be sufficient. Therefore, we suggest that modeling and role-playing of skills be used. Other useful means of training include reviewing films of parents with them while they are teaching social skills, pointing out do's and don'ts. Another equally important method is the "bug in the ear." With this strategy the parent wears a small receiver in the ear while working with the child. The parent can be prompted by the professional, who is seated on the other side of a one-way mirror. We have found this approach to be a useful and effective one, particularly since immediate feedback can be given on performance.

A final general point should be made with regard to parent training. Teaching skills should not be the only focus of training. It is recommended that the professional be available to provide emotional support and technical assistance above and beyond a structured learning program.

SUMMARY

In this final chapter we have attempted to point out that mentally retarded, visual-impaired, and hearing-impaired children can also benefit from social skills training. However, it should be emphasized that for optional effects various modifications in training are required for these special children. Given the extreme importance of social skills, training by psychologists and educators must be bolstered by efforts at school and at home. The behaviors targeted for intervention and the assessment and treatment procedures described earlier in this book should prove useful as starting points. Of course, appropriate adaptations are necessary. Much is yet to be done to further enhance social skills training with these children. However, as the reader can see, there are a number of currently available strategies which should prove useful in assisting such children. Continued work in this area should be encouraged and may well represent the "wave of the future." Surely, such efforts are warranted.

References

Achenbach, T. M., & Edelbrock, C. (1983). *Manual for the child behavior checklist and revised child behavior profile*. Vermont: Queen City Printers.

Andrasik, F., & Matson, J. L. (1985). Social skills training for the mentally retarded. In L. L'Abate & M. A. Milan (Eds.), *Handbook of social skills training and research*. New York: John Wiley & Sons, Inc.

Asher, S.R., Oden, S., & Gottman, J.M. (1977). Children's friendships in school settings. In L.G. Katz (Ed.), *Current topics in early childhood education*. (Vol.1). Norwood, NJ: Ablex.

Barclay, J.R. (1966). Interest patterns associated with measures of social desirability. *Personality Guidance Journal, 45*, 56—60.

Barton, E.S. (1973). Operant conditioning of appropriate and inappropriate social speech in the profoundly retarded. *Journal of Mental Deficiency Research, 17*, 183—191.

Beck, A.T., Rush, A.J., Shaw, B.F., et al. (1978). *Cognitive therapy of depression*. New York: The Guilford Press.

Bellack, A.S., Hersen, M., & Lamparski, D. (1979). Role-play tests for assessing social skills: Are they valid? Are they useful? *Journal of Consulting and Clinical Psychology, 47*, 335—342.

Bellack, A.S., Hersen, M., & Turner, S.M. (1978). Role-play tests for assessing social skills: Are they valid? *Behavior Therapy, 9*, 448—461.

Bernstein, D.A. (1973). Behavioral fear assessment: Anxiety or artifact? In H. Adams & I.P. Unikel (Eds.), *Issues and trends in behavior therapy*. Springfield, IL: Charles C. Thomas.

Bernstein, D.A., & Nietzel, M.T. (1977). Demand characteristics in behavior modification: The natural history of a "nuisance." In M. Hersen, R.M. Eisler, & P.M. Miller (Eds.), *Progress in behavior modification*, Vol.4. New York: Academic Press.

Bierman, K.L., & Furman, W. (1984). The effects of social skills training and peer involvement on the social adjustment of pre-adolescents. *Child Development, 55*, 151—162.

Billings, D.C., & Wasik, B.H. (985). Self-instructional training with preschooler: An attempt to replicate. *Journal of Applied Behavior Analysis, 18*, 61—67.

Borkovec, T.D. (1973). The effects of instructional suggestion and physiological cues on analogue fear. *Behavior Therapy, 4*, 185—192.

Bornstein, M.R., Bellack, A.S., & Hersen, M. (1977). Social-skills training for unassertive children: A multiple-baseline analysis. *Journal of Applied Behavior Analysis, 10*, 183—195.

Bornstein, P.H. (1985). Self-instructional training: A commentary and state-of-the-art. *Journal of Applied Behavior Analysis, 18*, 69—72.

Bornstein, P.H., & Quevillon, R.P. (1976). The effects of a self-instructional package on overactive preschool boys. *Journal of Applied Behavior Analysis, 9,* 179—188.

Bower, E.M. (1960). *Early identification of emotionally handicapped children in school.* Springfield, IL: Charles C. Thomas.

Brown, C. (1954). Factors affecting social acceptance of high school students. *School Review, 62,* 151—155.

Bryant, L.E., & Budd, K.S. (1984). Teaching behaviorally handicapped preschool children to share. *Journal of Applied Behavior Analysis, 17,* 45—46.

Christoff, K.A., Scott, W.O.N., Kelley, M.L., et al. (1985). Social skills and social problem training shy young adolescents. *Behavior Therapy, 16,* 468—477.

Clark, L., Gresham, F.M., & Elliott, S.N. (1985). Development and validation of a social skills assessment measure: The TROSS-C. *Journal of Psychoeducational Assessment, 4,* 347—358.

Combs, M.L., & Slaby, D.A. (1977). Social skills training with children. In B. Lahey and A.E. Kazdin (Eds.), *Advances in clinical child psychology.* (Vol.1). New York: Plenum Press.

Cowen, E.L. (1961). The experimental analogue: An approach to research in psychotherapy. *Psychological Reports, 8,* 9—10.

Cowen, E.L., Pederson, A., Babjian, H., et al. (1973). Long term follow-up of early detected vulnerable children. *Journal of Consulting and Clinical Psychology, 43,* 438—446.

Deluty, R.H. (1979). Children's action tendency scale: A self-report measure of aggressiveness, assertiveness, and submissiveness in children. *Journal of Consulting and Clinical Psychology, 47,* 1061—1071.

Deutsch, M., & Parks, L.A. (1978). The use of contingent music to increase appropriate conversational speech. *Mental Retardation, 16,* 33—36.

Dodge, K.A. (1980). Social cognition and children's aggressive behavior. *Child Development, 51,* 162—170.

Dunnington, M.J. (1957). Behavioral differences of sociometric status groups in a nursery school. *Child Development, 28,* 103—111.

Emery, R.E. (1982). Interparental conflict and the children of discord and divorce. *Psychological Bulletin, 92,* 310—330.

Farkas, G.M., Sherick, R.B., Matson, J.L., et al. (1981). Social skills training of a blind child through differential reinforcement. *The Behavior Therapist, 4,* 24—27.

Filipczak, J., Archer, M.B., Neale, M.S., et al. (1979). Issues in multivariate assessment of a large-scale behavioral program. *Journal of Applied Behavior Analysis, 12,* 593—613.

Fisher, D.C., & Wollersheim, J.P. (1986). Social reinforcement: A treatment component in verbal self-instruction training. *Journal of Abnormal Child Psychology, 14,* 41—48.

Forehand, R., Brody, G., & Smith, K. (1986). Contributions of child behavior and marital dissatisfaction to maternal perceptions of child maladjustment. *Behavior Research Therapy, 24,* 43—48.

Frame, C. & Matson, J.L. (1987). *Handbook of assessment in child psychopathology: Applied issues in differential diagnosis and treatment evaluation* New York: Plenum.

Francis, G., & Ollendick, T.N. (In press). Peer group entry behavior. *Child and Family Behavior Therapy.*

Froebel, F. (1903). *The education of man.* New York: Appleton.

Gardner, W.I., & Cole, C.L. (In press). Conduct problems. In C. Frame & J.L. Matson (Eds.), *Handbook of assessment in childhood psychopathology: Applied issues in differential diagnosis and treatment evaluation.* New York: Plenum.

Gottman, J. (1977). The effects of a modeling film on social isolation in preschool children: A methodological investigation. *Journal of Abnormal Child Psychology, 5.*

Greenspan, S. (1979). Social intelligence in the retarded. In N.R. Ellis (Ed.), *Handbook of*

Mental Deficiency: Psychological Theory and Research. (2nd ed.). Hillsdale, NJ: Erlbaum.

Gresham, F.M., Elliott, S.N., & Black. F.L. (1986). Factor structure replication and bias investigation of the teacher rating of social skills. Louisiana State University.

Gronlund, N.E. (1959). *Sociometry in the classroom*. New York: Harper & Row.

Grossman, H.J. (Ed.). (1983). *Manual on terminology and classification in mental retardation.* Washington D.C.: American Association on Mental Deficiency.

Guinouard, D.E., & Rychlak, J.F. (1982). Personality correlates of sociometric popularity in elementary school children. *Personnel and Guidance Journal, 40*, 438—442.

Harris, S.L. (1983). *Families of the developmentally disabled: A guide to behavioral interventions.* New York: Pergamon Press.

Hart, B.M., Reynolds, N.J., Baer, D.M., et al. (1986). Effect of contingent and noncontingent social reinforcement on the cooperative play of a preschool child. *Journal of Applied Behavior Analysis, 1*, 73—76.

Heinze, A., Matson, J.L., Helsel, W.J., et al. (In press). Assessing general psychopathology in visually handicapped children. *Australian and New Zealand Journal of Developmental Disabilities.*

Helsel, W.J., & Matson, J.C. (1984). The assessment of depression in children: The internal structure of the Child Depression Inventory (CDI). *Behaviour Research and Therapy, 22*, 289—298.

Herbert, J.F. (1901). *Outline of educational doctrine*. New York: Macmillan.

Hersen, M., & Bellack, A.S. (1976). A multiple baseline analysis of social skills training in chronic schizophrenics. *Journal of Applied Behavior Analysis, 9*, 239—245.

Higa, W.R., Tharp, R.G., & Calkins, R.P. (1979). Developmental verbal control of behaviors: Implications for self-control training. *Journal of Experimental Child Psychology, 26*, 489—497.

Hortshorne, H., May, M.A., & Maller, J.B. (1929). *Studies in the nature of character: II Studies in service and self-control*. New York: MacMillan.

Hymel, S., & Asher, S.R. (1977). Assessment and training of isolated children's social skills. Paper presented at the biennial meeting of the Society for Research in Child Development. New Orleans, Louisiana, March.

Jackson, H.J., & Brunder, J.N. (1986). Social validation of nonverbal behaviors in social skills training programs for adolescents — II. *Journal of Clinical Child Psychology, 15*, 50—54.

Kagan, L., & Moss, H.A. (1962). Birth to maturity: A study in psychological development New York: Wiley.

Kazdin, A.E. (1978). *History of behavior modification: Experimental foundations of contemporary research*. Baltimore, MD: University Park Press.

Kazdin, A.E. (1984). *Behavior modification in applied settings*. Homewood, IL: The Dorsey Press.

Kazdin, A.E., Esveldt-Dawson, K., & Matson, J.L. (1982). Changes in children's social performance as a function of preassessment experiences. *Journal of Clinical Child Psychology, 11*, 243—248.

Kazdin, A.E., & Matson, J.L. (1981). Solical validation with the mentally retarded. *Applied Research in Mental Retardation, 2*, 39—54.

Kazdin, A.E., Matson, J.L., & Esveldt-Dawson, K. (1981). Social skill performance among normal and psychiatric impatient children as a function of assessment conditions. *Behaviour Research and Therapy, 22*, 129—139.

Kazdin, A.E., Rodgers, A., & Colbus, D. (1986). The hopelessness scale for children: Psychometric characteristics and concurrent validity. *Journal of Consulting and Clinical Psychology, 54*, 241—245.

Kelly, J.A. (1982). *Social Skills training: A practical guide for interventions*. N York: Springer Publishing Company.

Kirk, S.A., & Johnson, G.O. (1951). *Educating the retarded child*. Cambridge, MA: Riverside Press.

Koegel, R.L., Russo,, D.C., & Rincover, A. (1977). Assessing and training teachers in the generalizatized use of behavior modification with autistic children. *Journal of Applied Behavior Analysis, 10,* 197—205.

Kohlberg, L. (1973). Continuities in childhood and adult moral development revisited. In P. Baltes and K.W. Schaie (Eds.), *Life-span developmental psychology*. New York: Academic Press.

Kohler, F.W., & Fowler, S.A. (1985). Training prosocial behaviors to young children: An analysis of reciprocity with untrained peers. *Journal of Applied Behavior Analysis, 18,* 187—200.

Kolstoe, O.P. (1976). *Teaching educable mentally retarded children*. (2nd ed.) New York: Holt, Rinehart and Wiston.

Koslin, B.L., Haarlow, R.N., Karlins, M.,et al. (1986). Predicting group status from member's cognitions. *Sociometry, 31,* 64—75.

La Greca, A.M. (1981). Peer acceptance: The correspondence between children's sociometric scores and teacher's ratings of peer interaction. Journal of Abnormal Child Psychology, 9, 167—178.

Lemanek, K.L., Williamson, D.A., Gresham, F.M., et al. (1986). Social skills training with hearing-impaired children and adolescents. *Behavior Modification, 10,*55—71.

Letherman, V.R., Williamson, D.A., Moddy, S.L., et al. (1982). Social skill assessment in children: Toward a socially valid instrument. Paper presented at the meeting of the *Association for the Advancement of Behavior Therapy*, Los Angeles, CA.

Lewinsohn, P.M. (1975). The behavioral study and treatment of depression. In M. Hersen, R. Eisler, & P.M. Miller (Eds.), *Progress in behavior modification*. New York: Academic Press.

Lewinsohn, P., & Graf, M. (1973). Pleasant activities and depression. *Journal of Abnormal Psychology, 79,* 291—295.

Lewinsohn, P.M., & Libet, J. (1972). Pleasant events, activity schedules, and depression. *Journal of Abnormal Psychology, 79,* 291—295.

Liberman, R.P., & Davis, J. (1975). Drugs and behavior analysis. In M. Hersen, R.M. Eisler, & P.M. Miller (Eds.), *Progress in behavior modification*. New York: Academic Press.

Liberman, R.P. Nuchterlein, K.H., & Wallace, C.J. (1982). Social skills training and the nature of schizophrenia. In J.P. Curran & P.M. Monti (Eds.), *Social skills training: A practical handbook for assessment and treatment*. New York: Guilford.

Luiselli, J.K., Colozzi, G., Donellon, S., et al. (1978). Training and generalization of a greeting exchange with a mentally retarded language-deficient child. *Education and Treatment of Children, 1,* 23—30.

MacDonald, M.L. (1982). Assertion training for women. In J.P. Curran & M.P. Monti (Eds.), *Social skills training: A practical handbook for assessment and treatment*. New York: Guilford.

Macklin, G.F., & Matson, J.L. (1985). A comparison of social behaviors among non-handicapped and hearing impaired children. *Behavior Disorders, 1,* 60—65.

MacMillan, D.L. (1982). *Mental retardation in school and society* (2nd Ed.). Boston: Little, Brown and Company.

Matson, J.L., & Breuning, S. (1983). *Assessing the Mentally Retarded*. New York: Grune and Stratton.

Matson, J.L., Esveldt-Dawson, K., Andrasik, F., et al. (1980). Direct observational and generalization effects of social skills training with emotionally disturbed children. *Behavior Therapy, 11,* 522—531.

Matson, J.L., Esveldt-Dawson, K., & Kazdin, A.E. (1981). Validation of methods for assessing social skills in children. *Journal of Clinical Child Psychology, 12,* 174—180.

Matson, J.L., Heinze, A., Helsel, W.J., et al. (1986). Assessing social behaviors in the visually handicapped. The Matson Evaluation of Social Skills with Youngsters (MESSY). *Journal of Clinical Child Psychology, 15,* 78—87.

Matson, J.L., & Helsel, W.J. (1986). Psychopathology of sensory-impaired children. In B. Lahey & A.E. Kazdin (Eds.), *Advances in Clinical Child Psychology,* New York: Plenum.

Matson, J.L., Kazdin, A.E., & Esveldt-Dawson, K. (1980). Training interpersonal skills among mentally retarded and socially dysfunctional children. *Behaviour Research and Therapy, 18,* 419—427.

Matson, J.L., Macklin, C.F., & Helsel, W.J. (1985). Psychometric properties of the Matson Evaluation of Social Skills with Youngsters (MESSY) with emotional problems and self concept in deaf children. *Journal of Behavior Therapy and Experimental Psychiatry, 16,* 117—123.

Matson, J.L., Manikam, R., Raymond, K., et al. (1987). Social skills training with autistic hearing-impaired children. Paper submitted for publication, Louisiana State University.

Matson, J.L. & Mulick, J.A. (1983). *Handbook of mental retardation.* New York: Pergamon.

Matson, J.L., Rotatori, A.F., & Helsel, W.J. (1983). Development of a rating scale to measure social skills in children: The Matson Evaluation of Social skills in children: The Matson Evaluation of Social Skills with Youngsters (MESSY). *Behaviour Research and Therapy, 21,* 335—340.

Matson, J.L., & Zeiss, R.A. (1979). The buddy system: A method for generalized reduction of inappropriate interpersonal behavior of retarded-psychiatric patients. *British Journal of Social and Clinical, 18,* 401—405.

McCandless, B.R., & Marshall, H.R. (1957). A picture sociometric technique for preschool children and its relation to teacher judgements of friendships. *Child Development, 28,*139—147.

McFall, R.M., & Lillesand, D.B. (1971). Behavior rehearsal with modeling and coaching in assertion training. *Journal of Abnormal Psychology, 77,* 313—323.

McFall, R.M. & Marston, A.R. (1970). An experimental investigation of behavior rehearsal in assertive training. *Journal of Abnormal Psychology, 76,* 295—303.

Meichenbaum, D.H. (1977). *Cognitive-behavior modification.* New York: Plenum Press.

Meichenbaum, D., & Goodman, J. (1971). Training impulsive children to talk to themselves: A means of developing self-control. *Journal of Abnormal Psychology, 77,* 115—126.

Michelson, L. Sugai, D.P., Wood, R.P., et al. (1983). *Social skill assessment and training with children.* New York: Plenum Press.

Miller, L.C. (1972). School Behavior Checklist: An Inventory of deviant behavior for elementary school children. *Journal of Consulting and Clinical Psychology, 38,* 134—144.

Moore, S.G., & Updegraff, R. (1984). Sociometric status of preschool children related to age, sex, nuturance giving and dependency. *Child Development, 35,* 519—524.

Moreno, J.L. (1953). *Who shall survive?* New York: Beacon House.

Nasby, W., Hayden, B., & DePaulo, B.M. (1980). Attributional bids among agressive boys to interpret revambiguous social stimuli as displays of hostility. *Journal of Abnormal Psychology, 89,* 459—468.

Nelson, R., Gibson, F. Jr., & Cutting, D.S. (1973). Videotaped modeling: The development of three appropriate social responses in a mildly retarded child. *Mental Retardation, 11,* 24—27.

Nelson, R.O., Hayes, S.C., Felton, J.C., et al. (1985). A comparison of data produced by different behavioral assessment techniques with implications for models of social-skills inadequacies. *Behavior Research and Therapy, 23,* 1—11.

Nihira, K., Foster, R., Shellhaas, W., et al. (1974). *AAMD Adaptive Behavior Scale Manual.* Washington: American Association on Mental Deficiency.

Nutter, D., & Reid, D.H. (1978). Teaching retarded women a clothing selection skill using community norms. *Journal of Applied Behavior Analysis, 11,* 475—487.

O'Leary, K.D., & Emery, R.E. (1985). Marital discord and child behavior problems. In D. Levine and P. Satz (Eds.), *Developmental variations and dysfunction*. Ne York: Academic Press.

Ollendick, T.H. (1982). The Social Competence Project. Unpublished manuscript. Virginia Polytechnic Institute and State University, Blacksburg.

Ollendick, T.H. (1984). Development and validation of the children's assertiveness inventory. *Child and Family Behavior Therapy, 5,* 1—15.

Ollendick, T.H., & Cerny, J.A. (1981). *Clinical behavior therapy with children*. New York: Plenum Press.

Ollendick, T.H., & Hersen, M. (1979). Social skills training for juvenile delinquents. *Behavior Research and therapy, 17,* 547—554.

Ollendick, T.H., & Hersen, M. (Eds.) (1983). *Handbook of child psychopathology*. New York: Plenum.

Ollendick, T.H., & Hersen, M. (1984). *Child behavioral assessment: Principles and procedures*. New York: Pergamon Press.

Olweus, D. (1979). Stability of aggressive reaction patterns in males: A review. *Psychological Bulletin, 86,* 852—875.

Patterson, G.R. (1964). An empirical approach to the classification of disturbed children. *Journal of Clinical Psychology, 20,* 326—337.

Payne, J.S., & Patton, J.R. (1981). *Mental Retardation*. Columbus, OH: Charles Merrill Publishing Company.

Piers, E.V., & Harris, D.B. (1964), *Piers-Harris Children's Self-Concept Scale*. California: Western Psychological Services.

Pravder, M.D., & Israel, A.C. (1983). The effect of peer influence systems on children's coercieve behavior. *Journal of Clinical Child Psychology, 12,* 145—152.

Puig-Antich, J. (1982). Major depression and conduct disorder in prepuberty. *Journal of the American Academy of Child Psychiatry, 21,* 18—128.

Putallaz, M., & Gottman, J.M. (1981). An interactional model of children's entry into peer groups. *Child Development, 52,*986—994.

Quay, H.C., & Peterson, D.R. (1975). *Manual for the behavior problem checklist*. Unpublished.

Rehm, L.P. (1977). A self-control model of depression. *Behavior Therapy, 8,* 787—804.

Reynolds, N.J., & Risley, T.R. (1968). The role of social and material reinforcers in increasing talking of a disadvantaged preschool child. *Journal of Applied Behavior Analysis, 1,* 253—262.

Richey, C.A. (1981). Assertiveness training for women. In S.P. Schinke (Ed.), *Behavioral methods in Social Welfare*. New York: Aldine.

Rickel, A.U., Eshelman, A.K., & Loigman, G.A. (1983). Social problem solving training. A follow-up study of cognitive and behavioral effects. *Journal of Abnormal Child Psychology, 11,* 15—28.

Rinn, R.C., & Markle, A. (1980). Modification of skill deficits in children. In A. S. Bellack & M. Hersen (Eds.), *Research and Practice in Social Skills Training*. New York: Plenum Press.

Robins, L.N. (1981). Epidemiological approches to natural history research. Antisocial disorders in children. *Journal of the American Academy of Child Psychiatry, 20,* 566—580.

Roff, M. (1961). Childhood social interactions and young adult bad conduct. *Journal of Abnormal and Social Psychology, 63,* 333—337.

Roff, M., Sell, B., & Golden, M.M. (1972). *Social adjustment and personality development in children*. Minneapolis: University of Minnesota Press.

Ross, D.M., & Ross, S.A. (1982). *Hyperactivity: Current issues, research and theory* (2nd ed.). New York: John Wiley & Sons.

Ruple, D.N., Parson, J.E., & Rose, J. (1976). Self-evaluative responses of children in an achievement setting. *Child Development*, 47, 990—997.

Sainato, D.M., Maheady, L., & Shook, G.L. (1986). The effects of a classroom management role on the social interaction patterns and social status of withdrawn kindergarten students. *Journal of Applied Behavior Analysis, 19,* 187—195.

Scanlon, E.M., & Ollendick, T.H. (1985). Children's assertive behavior: The reliability and validity of three self-report measures. *Child and Family Behavior Therapy, 7,* 9—21.

Schopler, E. (1978). Changing parental involvement in behavioral treatment. In M. Rutter & E. Schopler (Eds.), *Autism: A reappraisal of concepts and treatment.* New York: Plenum.

Shwartz, S., & Johnson, J.H. (1981). *Psychopathology of childhood: A clinical experimental approach.* New York: Pergamon Press.

Senatore, V., Matson, J.L., & Kazdin, A.E. (1982). A comparison of behavioral methods to train social skills to mentally retarded adults. *Behavior Therapy, 13,* 313—324.

Serna, L.A., Schumaker, J.B., Hazel, J.S., et al. (1986). Teaching reciprocal social skills training to parents and their delinquent adolescents. *Journal of Clinical Psychology,* 15,64—77.

Shechtman, A. (1970). Age patterns in children's psychiatric symptoms. *Child Development,* 41, 683—693.

Sherif, M., Harvey, O.J., White, B.J., et al. (1961). *Intergroup conflict and cooperation: The robber's cave experiment.* Norman, OK: University of Oklahoma.

Shure, M.B., Spivack, G., & Jaeger, M. (1971). Problem-solving thinking and adjustment among disadvantaged preschool children. *Child Development, 42,* 1791—1803.

Sisson, L.A., Van Hasselt, V.B., Hersen, M., et al. (1984). Increasing social behaviors in multihandicapped children through peer intervention. Unpublished manuscript, University of Pittsburgh.

Skinner, B.F. (1953). *Science and human behavior.* New York: The Free Press.

Spivack, G., & Shure, M. (1974). *Social adjustment of young children: A cognitive approach to solving real-life problems.* San Francisco: Jassey-Bass.

Swanson, H.L., Reinert, H.R. (1979). *Teaching strategies for children in conflict: Curriculum, methods, and materials* St. Louis: The C. V. Mosby Company.

Tygart, C.E. (1980). Student social structures and/or subcultures as factors in school crime: Toward a paradigm. *Adolescents, 15,* 13—22.

Ullman, C.A. (1975). Teachers, peers, and tests as predictors of adjustment. *Journal of Educational Psychology, 48,* 257—267.

Van Hasselt, V.B., Hersen, M., Whitehall, M.B., et al. (1979). Social skill assessment and training for children: An evaluative review. *Behaviour Research and Therapy, 17,* 413—417.

Van Hasselt, V.B., Kazdin, A.E., Hersen, M., (1985). A behavioral-analytic model for assessing social skills in blind adolescents. *Behaviour Research and Therapy, 23,* 395—405.

Walder, L.O., Aberson, R.P., Eron, L.D., et al. (1961). Development of a peer-rating measure of aggression. *Psychological Reports, 9,* 497—556.

Walls, R.T., Warner, T.J., Bacon, A., et al. (1977). Behavior checklists. In J.D. Cone & R.H. Kawkins (Eds.), *Behavioral Assessment.* New York: Bruner/Mazer Inc.

Whitman, T.L., Mercurio, J.R., & Caponigri, . (1970). Development of social responses in two severely retarded children. *Journal of Applied Behavioral Analysis, 3,* 133—138.

Williamson, D.A., Moody, S.C., Granberry, S.W., et al. (1983). Citerion-related validity of a role-play social skills test for children. *Behavior Therapy, 14,* 466—481.

Zigler, E., & Phillips, L. (1962). Social competence and the process-reactive distinction in psychopathology. *Journal of Abnormal and Social Psychology, 65,*

Author Index

Subject Index

About the Authors

Johnny L. Matson is Professor of Psychology (Clinical) at Louisiana State University in Baton Rouge, Louisiana. In addition to this position he has held academic positions in the Department of Learning and Development at Northern Illinois University and in the Departments of Psychiatry and Psychology (Clinical) at the University of Pittsburgh. He has also served as Program Director for the Jemison Center at Partlow State School and Hospital for mentally retarded persons in Tuscaloosa, Alabama. Dr. Matson has over 200 publications including 15 books, one of which, the *Handbook of Mental Retardation*, won the award as the best book in the social and behavioral sciences for 1983 awarded by the American Association of Publishers. He has been on the editorial board of several journals including the *Journal of Educational Psychology, Behavior Therapy, Journal of Clinical Child Psychology, Journal of Applied Behavior Analysis, Mental Retardation, Psychotherapy, Scandinavian Journal of Behavior Therapy* and the *Australian and New Zealand Journal of Developmental Disabilities*. He is the editor of *Research in Developmental Disabilities*. He has held national offices in several organizations including Coordinator of Membership Affairs for the Association for Advancement of Behavior Therapy and president of the mental retardation division of the American Psychological Association. His research interests include the assessment, diagnosis and treatment of problems of children and the developmentally disabled.

Thomas H. Ollendick (PhD, Purdue University, 1971) is currently Professor of Psychology and Director of Clinical Training at Virginia Polytechnic Institute and State University. He has formerly held positions at the Devereux Foundation, Indiana State University, and Western Psychiatric Institute and Clinic. He has co-authored *Clinical Behavior Therapy with children* (Plenum, 1981) with Jerome Cerny and co-edited the *Handbook of Child Psychopology* (Plenum, 1983) and *Child Behavioral Assessment: Principles and Procedures* (Pergamon, 1984), both with Michel

Hersen. The author of over 100 research articles and chapters, he is currently on the editorial board of six journals: *Research in Developmental Disabilities, Behavior Modification, Child and Family Behavior Therapy, Journal of Psychopathology and Behavioral Assessment, Journal of Clinical Child Psychology,* and the *Journal of Anxiety Disorders.* He also serves as an International Consultant for *Behaviour Change,* the official journal of the Australian Behaviour Modification Association. In addition, Dr Ollendick is the Coordinator of Convention Affairs for the Association for Advancement of Behavior Therapy, a Representative-at-Large for APA's Division 12, Section I on Clinical Child Psychology, and a member of NIMH's Psychosocial and Biobehavioral Treatments Subcommittee. He is the research recipient of a large-scale grant examining the efficacy of social skills training for "at risk" aggressive and withdrawn children.

Psychology Practitioner
Guidebooks

Editors
Arnold P. Goldstein, Syracuse University
Leonard Krasner, Stanford University & SUNY at Stony Brook
Sol L. Garfield, Washington University

Michael C. Roberts — PEDIATRIC PSYCHOLOGY: Psychological
 Interventions and Strategies for Pediatric Problems
Daniel S. Kirschenbaum, William G. Johnson & Peter M. Stalonas, Jr.
 — TREATING CHILDHOOD AND ADOLESCENT OBESITY
W. Stewart Agras — EATING DISORDERS: Management of Obesity,
 Bulimia and Anorexia Nervosa
Ian H. Gotlib & Catherine A. Colby — TREATMENT OF
 DEPRESSION : An Interpersonal Systems Approach
Walter B. Pryzwansky & Robert N. Wendt — PSYCHOLOGY AS A
 PROFESSION: Foundations of Practice
Cynthia D. Belar, William W. Deardorff & Karen E. Kelly — THE
 PRACTICE OF CLINICAL HEALTH PSYCHOLOGY
Paul Karoly & Mark P. Jensen — MULTIMETHOD ASSESSMENT OF
 CHRONIC PAIN
William L. Golden, E. Thomas Dowd & Fred Friedberg —
 HYPNOTHERAPY: A Modern Approach
Patricia Lacks — BEHAVIORAL TREATMENT FOR PERSISTENT
 INSOMNIA
Arnold P. Goldstein & Harold Keller — AGGRESSIVE BEHAVIOR:
 Assessment and Intervention
C. Eugene Walker, Barbara L. Bonner & Keith L. Kaufman — THE
 PHYSICALLY AND SEXUALLY ABUSED CHILD: Evaluation and
 Treatment
Robert E. Becker, Richard G. Heimberg & Alan S. Bellack — SOCIAL
 SKILLS TRAINING TREATMENT FOR DEPRESSION
Richard F. Dangel & Richard A. Polster — TEACHING CHILD
 MANAGEMENT SKILLS
Albert Ellis, John F. McInerney, Raymond DiGiuseppe & Raymond
 Yeager — RATIONAL-EMOTIVE THERAPY WITH ALCOHOLICS
 AND SUBSTANCE ABUSERS
Johnny L. Matson & Thomas H. Ollendick — ENHANCING
 CHILDREN'S SOCIAL SKILLS: Assessment and Training
Edward B. Blanchard, John E. Martin & Patricia M. Dubbert — NON-
 DRUG TREATMENTS FOR ESSENTIAL HYPERTENSION
Samuel M. Turner & Deborah C. Beidel — TREATING OBSESSIVE-
 COMPULSIVE DISORDER